RETURN TO
CORRIEBUSH

Stories and recipe
LYNN BEDFOR
ILLUSTRATED BY TONY

Author's Acknowledgements

Just when I thought I'd finally finished my book – dotted the i's, crossed the t's, checked, double-checked, made changes and proof-read – just when I thought it was all ready to go and my weary PC and I could finally shut down, Joy Clack reminded me that I had yet to submit the Author's Acknowledgements. "But don't panic, you can keep it short," she soothed. Now how do I do that? I can't simply say thank you Linda, Joy, Bev and Tony, can I? If Linda had not approved my manuscript, if Joy had not contributed her absolutely impeccable editing, enthusiasm and constant encouragement, if Bev had not used her designer talents with such energy and excellence, if Tony had not captured the characters and events with so much insight and craft, if all this team – who have become very dear to me – had not worked so tirelessly to produce the book as you now see it – there simply would be no book.

So Thank You seems to me totally inadequate. But Joy says I have to keep this short.

So Thank You it is – but you won't believe how deeply I feel it. **LYNN**

First published in 2005 by Struik Publishers
(a division of New Holland Publishing
(South Africa) (Pty) Ltd)
Cape Town • London • Sydney • Auckland
www.struik.co.za

Cornelis Struik House, 80 McKenzie Street, Cape
Town 8001, South Africa
Garfield House, 86–88 Edgware Road, London
W2 2EA, United Kingdom
14 Aquatic Drive, Frenchs Forest,
NSW 2086, Australia
218 Lake Road, Northcote,
Auckland, New Zealand

New Holland Publishing is a member of Johnnic
Communications Ltd

1 2 3 4 5 6 7 8 9 10

Publishing Manager: Linda de Villiers
Editor: Joy Clack
Designer: Beverley Dodd
Illustrator: Tony Grogan
Proofreader: Irma van Wyk

Reproduction by Hirt & Carter Cape (Pty) Ltd
Printed and bound by Craft (Pte) Ltd,
Singapore

ISBN 1 77007 212 8

IMAGES OF AFRICA
PHOTO LIBRARY

Log on to our photographic website
www.imagesofafrica.co.za

Contents

Author's Introduction

When I wrote *Fig Jam and Foxtrot* – a collection of fictitious stories about women living in a small town which I named Corriebush – I concluded the introduction with these words: '… all the people … have gone. But perhaps their ghosts still wander about Corriebush, for it's a place that is not easy to leave or forget.' At the time, I thought that was it. An end to my rambling through the mists of my childhood, inventing people and circumstances that allowed me to re-enter my years of growing up in a village in the Karoo; to share it, and in so doing to put it to bed. I was wrong. Corriebush refuses to be abandoned. It demanded that I return; my six protagonists, my six whacky women, would not go away. And so here they have surfaced again: Maria and Anna, Sophia and Nellie, Amelia and Lily. Six gentle, kind-hearted but nosey women who loved nothing better than tea and gossip. They presented me with four more stories.

I have interspersed them with a collection of my recipes – some new, some revised, and some from previous works that simply did not want to be forgotten, like Corriebush. I look back now, searching for a reason – and perhaps it lies in the fact that I seemed to grow up in a never-ending summer of content.

I believe that many people who have grown up in the Karoo will identify with this feeling, even if it is coloured with the sentiment that comes with the passage of time. Nevertheless, I stay with my childhood dreams and the memory of waking up each morning as the sun rose over the mountain, scalding the bushes and washing the kloofs in a fury of colour. The glow was reflected into my bedroom; it bounced off the walls and painted my eiderdown – which was covered in green chintz with those old-fashioned pink roses.

Ahead of me lay one magical hour before school started – the hour in which the town stretched and stirred into life. I would fetch my bicycle – clumsy old balloon tyres and clunking chain – and pedal through the streets that wound up to the flanks of the berg. The air was new and fresh, the oak trees thrummed with morning birds, and the town was mine alone. Down the avenue of purple jacarandas I flew, past the butcher's house – fleshy red biltong strung out on his verandah – past the ivy-smothered cottage where the mad woman lived (they said she danced on moonlit nights, stark naked under her fig tree), and when I heard the yawn of early-morning voices and shutters being opened – *doef* – as they hit the walls, I would head for home and breakfast.

This was how most days started, and usually ended with my parents and me taking an evening stroll through the slumbering streets, now relieved of heat and shadowed in the cool evening air. We would say goodnight to everyone sitting on their stoeps, drinking coffee, the men puffing on their pipes, quietly contemplating the swelter of the day and the welcome grumble of thunder behind the mountain. And when I slipped into bed I slept peacefully, knowing that my home town was special; the people eternal.

That's how it was. And that's how it is with Corriebush.

Jacoba

The morning was cold, the mountain above Corriebush lightly iced with snow. '*Sjoe!*' puffed Lily. 'Just look at the steam coming out of my mouth. '*Sjoe!*' she puffed again. 'I'm smoking like a pipe.' She wrapped her yellow scarf tightly round her neck; rubbed her gloved hands together. 'My fingers have all gone to sleep.'

'And the train's *blerrie* late,' complained Sophia.

'Perhaps she's not even on it,' remarked Nellie. 'Missed the connection. You know how these young people are, especially when they're famous.'

'I just hope she's been sensible and remembered to dress for the Karoo in July,' went on Amelia. 'Corriebush isn't Hawaii, you know.'

'Isn't that a little white puff in the sky?' asked Maria. 'Look, over there! Just above the koppie beyond Van Wyk's dairy.'

'*Ja-nee*, that's smoke alright,' agreed Anna.

'And together they turned their heads and stared into the middle distance.

The Welcoming Committee had come to the station much too early, because the train from the north seldom arrived according to schedule. It all depended on how many cows were in milk. If all the neighbouring farmers were having a good season, there were several stops to be made in order to load the full cans. If there were no cans at the farm gates, the train just rattled past. So one never knew. And that was why they had come early and, for a good hour, had stood side-by-side outside the ticket office, clucking about the weather, anxiously peering this way and that, teetering a little on their high heels like birds on a telephone wire. They were not given to early rising in winter, did not enjoy standing on the station in the biting easterly wind, but as Nellie said, they had no right to complain. 'How would we feel, after all, if *we* were Jacoba van Rhyn? If *we* were famous and coming back to visit our home town out of the kindness of our hearts, how would we feel if there was no-one to welcome us and say "Hello" and "How Are You?"'

'Nellie, you're right,' agreed Sophia. 'What does a bit of standing around matter, when it's such a suspicious occasion?'

'*Auspicious*, Sophia.'

'A first for Corriebush.'

'A once-off. Never to be repeated.'

'What if fame has gone to her head and she walks right past us and into a taxi?'

'Never. Not our Jacoba. She might be a star now, but she was always a sweet, polite child and she won't have changed. I can feel it in my waters, as my mother used to say. Basically, she'll still be our own little Jacoba van Rhyn, come home to roost for a while.'

'Preen her feathers a bit.'

'Show Corriebush a thing or two.'

'Nothing wrong with that.'

'She'll probably be dressed up, though. After all, when you've been to Russia and seen all those churches and museums and palaces, you don't walk round in flat shoes anymore.'

'So what will she be wearing, I wonder?'

'Oh furs, that's for sure. Furs and fine leather boots. Jewels too.'

'A Brown Bear hat on her head,' added Amelia, looking wise.

'That's right. A Brown Bear hat,' they echoed.

'And a muff right up to her elbows.'

'That too.'

'Now remember, she may be so dolled up that we don't recognise her, but if we all shout "Yoo-hoo!" as she climbs down the steps, she'll be sure to notice us.'

'Get ready, then. I see the engine's coming round the bend.'

Like a flock of long-necked geese they peered down the line, still chattering excitedly. But when Jacoba stepped onto the platform, a silence fell as suddenly as though a blanket had been thrown over a cage of canaries.

Soon after matriculating, Jacoba van Rhyn had left Corriebush for Port Elizabeth, as had many of her friends. But in Jacoba's case it wasn't the bright lights that beckoned. Music was her passion, and she had been accepted as a pianoforte student at a leading college of music in the city.

The women had been astonished by her decision.

'I really thought it was Hollywood for her.'

'A Miss World in the making.'

'A bride fit for a king!'

'And who does she choose? Chopin.'

If Jacoba had not been such a lovely young woman, her choice of career would not have caused such surprise. But the trouble was, Jacoba was absolutely stunning. Although her parents, Geo and Joey, were quite an ordinary-looking couple, their only child had inherited the best genes from both sides.

'A flawless beauty, that one,' the women often remarked. 'Flawless, with a nature to match.'

'Not high and mighty either.'

'Nor hoity-toity, like some of the other good-lookers.'

In spite of the fact that she had been elected Spring Queen in her final school year, and had every young man in the district asking for a date, Jacoba remained sweetly shy and seemingly unaware of the admiring looks she received wherever she went. Her hair was long, very long, blonde streaked over brown, her skin a pale ivory, her eyes startling sea-green under arched black brows. Added to this were the blessings of long shapely legs and generous breasts, which made her waist seem even smaller, her hips rounder.

'There's a model there,' the women told Joey.

'Send her to Milan and you can retire.'

But all Jacoba wanted to do was play the piano. She was awarded honours for all her examinations, right up to the Licentiate Division, when she faultlessly played Liszt's lyrical Consolation No. 6.

'She seems to go into another world,' Joey told them. 'When she's playing I can drop an empty bucket behind her and she won't even hear it.'

'Old soul,' remarked Daniel, who knew about these things.

Although Geo and Joey had to get a loan from the bank, they did not try to dissuade their daughter from studying further. They paid her fees and found safe lodgings for her in a boarding house in Port Elizabeth. It was close to the college, and there was a piano in the dining room. It stood next to the dessert trolley and Mrs Parks, the owner, said she was welcome to use it.

'Never had a finger on it since old Mr Jingles died. His real name was Arthur, but we all called him Mr Jingles because he used to play while we had our meals. Tickled the ivories, as they say. All the old tunes. Sometimes people even got up and did a foxtrot or two. It will be good to have some music in here again.'

Jacoba couldn't play a foxtrot, but at the evening meals she introduced them to Beethoven and Brahms, Tchaikovsky and Schumann and the elderly boarders would sit spellbound, heads cocked to one side, forks poised, forgetting to eat, focused on the beautiful girl, mesmerised by the music.

After just one year, Jacoba was giving solo recitals in the City Hall. And this was when the unbelievable, unforeseeable happened.

She was scheduled to play two works by Schumann, *Des Abends* and *Soaring*, followed by Grieg's *Sonata in E minor* after the interval, and posters went up all over the city. The advertising was clever: the posters featured a romantic photograph of the young pianist with the flowing hair, perfect profile, bent over the keys, wearing a long, white evening gown. Predictably, every ticket was sold within days, including one to Richard Evans.

As a scout for the Carter Trust, Richard wasn't particularly interested in music. His job was to fly the world in search of talent. Richard was a nephew of Edward Carter, a wealthy philanthropist who, before his death, had set up a trust fund with the young man as executor. 'This is my aim and it will be your mission, Richard,' he had told him, and then dictated these exact words: 'The Carter Trust will embrace the fields of music, art and literature. It will honour young women with both beauty and intelligence, who would use the prize money not only to further their talents, but to enhance the lives of others less fortunate.' Each year the venue for the competition was held in a different country. That year it was Russia.

After Jacoba's performance in Port Elizabeth, Richard went backstage, introduced himself, asked her a few details and explained his mission. Richard was glib and experienced and he knew that, however much Jacoba might waver, he held the trump card. If she won she would get a great deal of prize money, she could reimburse her parents for her fees and she could bring music to the children of Corriebush; even teach some of them how to play.

'You could set up a music school, fill it with instruments, and bring much happiness into other people's lives.' Seeing Jacoba's hesitation, he knew how to hit the final chord.

'Perhaps this is your vocation, Jacoba. Your chance to give back some of the blessings with which you have been endowed.'

Richard had gauged her nature correctly. He knew she would capitulate, and she did. But he couldn't resist a barb about her name. 'I wish, though, that you had another name.'

'Like what?'

'Like – like Opal, for example. Or even Rosemary, just as a stage name. But *Jacoba?*'

Jacoba wouldn't hear of it. 'If the name was good enough for my grandmother, then it's good enough for me.'

The details that followed terrified her. 'This year the competition will be in Russia – Moscow, to be exact. You will fly over next week, and this will give you just one month to practise there and meet the other contestants – there will be several pianists, a cellist, at least one violinist, as well as artists, poets and authors. There will be both scheduled and unscheduled performances for the musicians; the artists can expect workshops and exhibitions; and there will be reading and practicals for the poets and authors. All the contestants will also have several interviews with the judges. One month will give you time to acclimatise to the weather, buy some appropriate clothes and pay a few visits to a beauty parlour before your final performance. Remember, the judges will be looking not only for ability and dedication, but also for poise, intelligence and grace. You should score highly and I wish you luck.'

Geo and Joey were not happy about allowing their nineteen-year-old daughter to travel so far away, but they were proud of her having been chosen, and realised it was an exceptional opportunity. Richard actually wrote to reassure them that 'all the girls', as he put it, would be well managed and taken care of, and in the end they sent her off with their blessing, a hot water bottle and sheepskin gloves tucked into her suitcase.

'You say the child is going to RUSSIA?' exclaimed Sophia, when Joey broke the news at tea one afternoon.

'Yes, to Moscow.'

'Oh my glory. Well, at least it's not Blerrievostok.'

'*Vladisvostok*, Sophia.'

'I once had a lovely boyfriend who joined a Russian ship. He was a deck-hand, you know, out to see the world on the cheap. And they sailed to Blerrievostok and when they parked in the harbour he ran away and was never heard of again.'

'*Ag* fie.'

Sophia dabbed at her eyes. 'Clean gone.'

Jacoba shivered as she unpacked in the modest hotel room in Moscow. She had met

the other contestants, could not understand all the different languages, but she knew that in any case they would all be too busy to socialise much. And so it was. Every day, for most of the day, they practised their art. Jacoba spent at least eight hours at the piano, hardly taking time off to eat. She lost weight, because when she wasn't at the piano, she would sit in her room brooding. And because she was so weary, physically, her confidence had plummeted. By day her thoughts kept turning to the heart-thumping performance that lay ahead; her nights were haunted by nightmares of what might happen. It helped a little to write these things down in her diary. 'It's that final, hushed moment when I sit down on the piano stool; the terrible, inevitability of it! No escape. My mind a blank. I sit staring at the keys. Then I fumble, stumble, sharps instead of flats, I'm in a minor key instead of a major, I hesitate, start again … stand before the judges, answer questions … If only it were over, finished, home again, gone … Why did I come?' Often she cried herself to sleep. And yet, and yet … on the night of the performance, when she sat down to play, from the very first note Jacoba lost all her fears; forgot where she was; allowed the notes to float under her fingers, now soft and slow, then forte and joyous. Once again she was in the dream world that artists enter when they become one with creation. Her performance was brilliant.

Once the news had been telegraphed to the *Corriebush Daily*, it spread through the town like a veld fire. 'JACOBA TRIUMPHS!' read the headlines. 'OUR DAUGHTER OF THE VELD, OUR GEM OF THE KAROO, BRINGS GLORY TO CORRIEBUSH!'

Geo and Joey were ecstatic. Joey could not stop crying. In the end the women had to forbid her to come to the station. 'After all, this is a joyous occasion, Joey, and we know she's your child and all, but we can't have you sniffling there. We're going to clap and call Yoo-hoo when she arrives. And you'd be a sorry sight, blowing your nose all the time.'

And so that is the story, and the reason why the Welcoming Committee of Corriebush – Anna and Lily and Maria and Nellie and Amelia and Sophia – came to be standing on the station platform so early one biting July morning.

Jacoba jumped from the train onto the platform and that was when a shocked silence fell on them. There were no furs, and no jewels. Jacoba was wearing jeans, a turtle-neck sweater and tackies. Their smiles drooped briefly, but then she held out her arms. 'Aunties!' and quickly they came to their senses, rushed to embrace her. It was an emotional

Jacoba 15

moment for them, they were all choked up, now laughing, now reaching for their handkerchiefs. Sophia was the first to find her voice.

'Where's your yak hat, then?'

'My *what*?'

'*Ag* child, never mind,' said Lily, embarrassed. 'We'll explain another day. Right now Herman is waiting with the car over there under the pepper tree. And your parents have put the kettle on. Come! We'll all help you with your things.'

They drove to Geo and Joey's smallholding just outside the town.

Lily raised her cup of tea. 'To Jacoba!'

'To Jacoba!'

Joey cut the cake. 'The whole of Corriebush is buzzing with plans to celebrate you, my child. We thought perhaps a big party in the Town Hall? Such an award needs to be honoured, not so ladies?'

They nodded furiously, but Jacoba held up her hand.

'*Ja* , I won the award, but the whole point is to try and double the prize money now. It's my duty.'

'*Ag*, the child wants to do her bit by the community.'

'That's right, Auntie Maria. That's exactly what I *have* to do. So we must think of a plan.'

'A bazaar?' suggested Sophia.

'*Ag* no, not enough profit there.'

'A raffle then?'

'Still not good enough.'

They went home to think, and it was Servaas who came up with a sensational idea.

'A float procession!' he exclaimed. 'Like they have at the universities. Lorries cruising down the street, all decorated with streamers and things, and you ladies standing on them shaking tins.

All our friends will line the streets and throw money at you.'

Maria presented the idea to all the women at a tea the following afternoon. Jacoba loved it.

But Lily had reservations. 'We have to have a theme,' she told them, remembering her days at University, when she had been Carmen Miranda with a bowl of fruit on her head. 'You can't just have lorries looking like birthday cakes, there must be something more, to encourage people to *give*.'

They stirred their tea thoughtfully; nibbled the cookies; said 'I just can't think of a thing,' and 'I'm no good at this sort of game,' when Jacoba suddenly jumped up. 'I've got it! I've got it! We'll have a "Guess-who? Fancy Dress!"'

'Brilliant!' Amelia exclaimed. 'Absolutely the jackpot! And seeing that the money is for children, why don't we each dress up as a character from a children's story?'

'Or a fairytale! Or a myth!'

Their enthusiasm started to sparkle.

'And there'll be six lorries – we'll borrow them from the sheep farmers, they all have big lorries with railings round – and each of us will be on a lorry with a tin up front for donations, and a tin at the back for entry forms.'

'Entry forms?'

'*Ja*, people will have to guess who we are, and the first one drawn with all the correct answers will get a prize. Perhaps one of the farmers will donate a sheep.'

The women whooped with excitement. The plan was faultless and fun, and they rushed home to consult their husbands and all the old story books in their dusty bookcases, promising to meet again the following morning to discuss their decisions.

They sat round Amelia's dining table – they had decided to meet there because Daniel was known to be the brains among the men and might come up with some great suggestions. Lily set the ball rolling. 'I'm going to be the siren of the Rhine, sitting on the Lorelei,' she announced proudly.

'Sitting on *what*?'

'A rock.'

'That's nice,' said Sophia.

'Yes. The siren sat on a steep rock called the Lorelei, on the bank of the river, and sang songs that lured sailors to her and then they died.'

'*Ag* fie.'

'So Herman will build a little rock for me and I'll sit on it, undo my bun so that my hair hangs down, and I'll beckon and sing 'Ich Weiss Nicht' – that one. I might even drape a fish across my lap if old Vissie the Fishmonger has a good catch that day, a yellowtail perhaps, to give them a clue.'

'A tricky one, Lily. A tricky one that. But very original.'

Maria chose to be Cinderella. 'Simple. I'll just stick some patches onto my blue ball gown – you know the one I wore to the Show Ball and Servaas put his foot right through the skirt in the foxtrot? It's spoilt anyway. Then I'll tie an apron round my waist and sweep the lorry floor with a broom and hold my hand to my forehead and look very sad and hungry and faint.'

'Now I don't wish to sound vain,' said Anna, 'but I'd like to be The Sleeping Beauty. James will make up a nice soft bed for me, and I'll just lie down in a pretty pink nightdress, with a crown on my head and my little canary on my chest. Maybe, after a while, I'll give a big yawn, and sit up and look about me, very confused. That will give them a clue alright.'

Both Nellie and Amelia chose quickly guessable ones, to encourage the children to support. 'Red Riding Hood for me,' said Nellie. 'I'll wear a red scarf round my head and Charlie's big red mackintosh, and I'll tuck a basketful of goodies under my arm. Charlie can put a potted tree on the back of the lorry, to look like a forest, and I'll walk round and round it, and now and then I'll dip into my basket, throw a biscuit to a child and ask for a tickey or a sixpence for my box, in payment.'

Amelia would be a perfect Goldilocks. Not only did she have truly flaxen hair, but she was short and girlish and plump. She'd sit at a table on her lorry, surrounded by three teddy bears of just the right size – father, mother and baby bear, which she would borrow from Tom at the ToyShopStop. 'I'll put three bowls of porridge, a jug of milk and a jar of honey on the table, and from the time the lorries take off, I'll start eating. I'll go on until all three plates are empty, and then I'll press the buttons in the backs of the bears and they'll growl. The children will love it.'

'Your turn, now Sophia.'

'Olive.'

'Olive?'

'That's what I said.'

'But I don't know of a fairy tale with an olive – do you, Lily?'

'Never heard of one. Is it just *Olive* Sophia? Or does it have a surname?'

'Olive's Twist,' Sophia replied smugly.

'Oh dear, Sophia, it's *Oliver* Twist and that's a *whole novel!*'

'Oh my glory. Well then I'll be Olive Schreiner.'

They began to look desperate. 'She's not a fairy tale, Sophia.'

'Then it's Olive Oyl for me.'

'Olive Oyl?'

Jacoba 19

'*Ja*, Popeye's wife. You know, the one who ate the spinach.'

It was no use arguing further, except to ask her how she was going to look like an olive.

'There's an old rain barrel in our back yard, a round belly and narrower top and bottom, it will look just like an olive once Dawid has painted it green. Then I'll sit inside with a bunch of spinach sticking out of the top, and Bob's your uncle. I'm Olive Oyl.'

The float procession was scheduled for the following Saturday morning, as most of the farmers came to town on Saturdays. The mayor and town councillors had promised their support, and the shopkeepers had agreed to close their doors for the duration so that their staff and would-be shoppers could help swell the crowds and toss up their money. And, of course, being a Saturday, all the school children and their teachers would be free and able to cheer them on.

It was a glorious sight. Slowly the lorries rumbled their way down the main street, then down towards the mountain, and up to the houses on the hill – the elite area. The men had gone to heaps of trouble to brighten up the old, rather weary farm lorries, for the planks had been scratched by a million hooves over the years. They draped them with streamers and calendulas and nasturtiums, which grew in every garden in Corriebush, because they were hardy and did not need much rain. They wound ivy leaves round every possible wheel, strut, axle and cab, twisted streamers into the wooden rails, and tied big bunches of balloons on the backs, so that they would dip and rise in the breeze. The tins, painted in bright colours, were hung in prominent positions.

The Corriebush Carnival was a total, hooting success. People dropped coins not only into the tins, they threw them onto the lorries as well.

'*Sjoe!* On my *blerrie* head,' wailed Sophia as a half-crown struck her forehead. Some farmers thrust notes into the tins, others stuffed in their cheques, and everyone entered for the prize draw, except the husbands who said it would be a *skelm* thing to do because they all knew who their wives were. In the end, Vissie won the prize, and the total donations amounted to close on £1,800.

Jacoba was ecstatic. Even after paying her parents for her fees, she had enough over to hire a hall, buy an upright piano, two violas, a trumpet, a triangle and two recorders. For six months she stayed in Corriebush and in that time the thrall of classical music touched 45 pupils of all races. They left their rugby and marbles, their tricycles, bicycles, even their dolls. And in no time she had a little orchestra going, holding concerts for all the parents.

Before long, however, Jacoba had to go back to the college to continue her studies, but she promised to return once a month for further rehearsals and tuition. In the end, the Corriebush Children's Orchestra was playing all over the district, as far away as Graaff-Reinet and beyond. After five years, during which time Jacoba never missed a single monthly visit, she finally had to stop. Her classes had increased to 70, but she had married a Port Elizabeth doctor and felt it was time to stay at home. Geo and Joey became the proud grandparents of four boys, including a set of triplets.

Corriebush will never forget Jacoba: there's a plaque on the wall outside the little hall in which she taught, and on it is written simply:

JACOBA'S MUSIC SCHOOL

It might still be there, just past the museum, in the avenue lined with oak trees.

Starters

Mushroom Mountains

When you're nervous about the merits – or quantities – of your main course, it's sensible to turn to a robust starter so that whatever happens afterwards, the meal would, at least, have got off to a fulsome start. This recipe is a good choice on such an occasion: large mushrooms stuffed to bursting, nestled on a bed of rocket and served with a herby, buttery baguette. All delicious, assembled in minutes, and virtually everything can be done in advance.

6 jumbo brown mushrooms (400 g)
(sometimes called 'braai' mushrooms)
fresh basil leaves
½ onion, coarsely grated
3 cloves garlic, crushed
firm but ripe tomatoes
sea salt and sugar
mozzarella cheese, sliced
dried oregano
olive oil
milled black pepper
rocket leaves

Slice the stems off the mushrooms and arrange the caps, hollows up, in a large, lightly oiled baking dish, then do the stuffing bit, one at a time, as follows: First a generous sprinkling of basil, cover with onion, crush the garlic over (divide equally), top with a thick slice of tomato, sprinkle the tomato (not the mushroom) with salt and sugar, cover with cheese, sprinkle with a few pinches of oregano, drizzle each mountain with 10–15 ml (2–3 tsp) olive oil and finish with a few grindings of black pepper. If working ahead, cover and refrigerate, but allow to return to room temperature before baking, uncovered, at 180 °C for about 30 minutes, until the mushrooms are soft and juicy, and the cheese has melted. Serve on a bed of rocket with the herbed French loaf. **Serves 6.**

Baked French Loaf with Fresh Herb Butter

Mash together: 250 g soft butter; 125 ml (½ cup) chopped spring onions plus tops; a small handful of chopped parsley; 6 sage leaves, chopped; 6 sprigs marjoram leaves chopped; 2 sprigs thyme leaves, chopped; 2 cloves garlic, crushed (optional); a pinch of salt. Slice one large, long French loaf in 12 mm thick slices to the base, but not right through. Butter between the slices. If it oozes out at the top, scrape it off and slap it in again. Wrap in foil, leaving only the top exposed, and bake with the mushrooms for the last 15 minutes. **Enough for 30–40 slices.**

Starter Spreads & Snacks

If your main course needs both last-minute attention and careful timing, serving a starter beforehand can be tricky. Rather serve snacks with the preprandial drinks. The following spreads (choose one fish, one mushroom), served on breads or crisp, savoury biscuits, are quick to prepare, always disappear in a flash, and only the crostini need last-minute heating.

Smoked Salmon Spread

120–160 g smoked salmon slices or offcuts

250 g smooth, low-fat cottage cheese

15 ml (1 Tbsp) fresh lemon juice

60 ml (4 Tbsp) very soft butter

a few drops of Tabasco sauce

5 ml (1 tsp) tomato paste (for colour)

a pinch each of sea salt and sugar (to taste)

milled black pepper

fresh dill to garnish

Place all the ingredients, except the pepper and garnish, in a processor fitted with the metal blade and process until smooth. Check seasoning, then spoon into a glass fridge container and refrigerate for a few hours. Spread thickly onto slices of crustless, lightly buttered rye or wholewheat bread, grind a little pepper over, slice into fingers and serve on a platter garnished with fresh dill. **Makes 500 ml (2 cups).**

Smoked Snoek Spread

200 g smoked snoek

250 g smooth, low-fat cottage cheese

15 ml (1 Tbsp) fresh lemon juice

60 ml (4 Tbsp) very soft butter

30 ml (2 Tbsp) sweet chilli sauce

30 ml (2 Tbsp) finely snipped chives

paprika

Remove all the dark skin from the snoek, carefully slip out *all* the bones, then flake finely, feeling between your fingers to make sure you've got rid of them all. Now you should have 150 g. Put into a bowl (not a processor) and add the rest of the ingredients, except the paprika. Mix well, using a wooden spoon. Taste. It may need a pinch of salt, and another 15 ml (1 Tbsp) chilli sauce. Spoon into a glass fridge container, cover and refrigerate for several hours or overnight. Spread generously on slices of crustless, lightly buttered wholewheat bread, dust with paprika and slice into fingers. **Makes about 500 ml (2 cups).**

Mushroom-Cream Cheese Spread

15 ml (1 Tbsp) each oil and butter

60 ml (¼ cup) sherry

15 ml (1 Tbsp) soy sauce

5 ml (1 tsp) chopped fresh rosemary leaves

2 cloves garlic, crushed

1 small onion, finely chopped

250 g button mushrooms, wiped and finely chopped

250 g cream cheese (use low-fat if preferred)

60 ml (4 Tbsp) chopped parsley

30 ml (2 Tbsp) snipped chives

a pinch of sugar

Heat the oil, butter, sherry, soy sauce, rosemary, garlic and onion in a frying pan. Add the mushrooms and sauté until soft and liquid absorbed, but still very moist. Remove from the stove, slowly stir in the cheese, then add the herbs and sugar. Taste to check the seasoning, then spoon into a glass container, cover and refrigerate for at least a few hours to allow the flavours to blend. Serve on savoury biscuits. **Makes 500 ml (2 cups).**

Mushroom Crostini

12–16 slices slightly stale bread

45 ml (3 Tbsp) oil and 20 ml (4 tsp) butter, melted together

extra 45 ml (3 Tbsp) butter

250 g button or brown mushrooms, wiped and very finely chopped

50 ml (3 Tbsp plus 1 tsp) flour

250 ml (1 cup) hot milk

6 spring onions, finely chopped

1 ml (¼ tsp) dried oregano

sea salt and milled black pepper

8 black olives, pitted and slivered

grated Parmesan or pecorino cheese

Slice the crusts off the bread and stamp out rounds using a 5–6 cm scone cutter. Place on a baking tray and brush both sides with the melted oil-butter mixture. Bake at 180 ℃ for 10–12 minutes, until crisp, turning once. Cool. Melt the extra butter in a saucepan, add the mushrooms and toss over low heat until *all* the liquid has evaporated. Sprinkle in the flour and, when absorbed, slowly add the milk. Bring to the boil and stir until very thick. Remove from the stove and add the spring onions, oregano and seasoning to taste. (If working ahead, cool, cover and refrigerate.) To bake, spread the mushroom mixture thickly on each round of bread, top with olives and sprinkle with cheese. Bake at 200 ℃ for 12–15 minutes until piping hot. **Makes about 36.**

Mini Cucumber Cheesecakes with Avocado

These crustless little cheesecakes make an unusual, minty, refreshing yet creamy hot-weather starter, which looks stunning turned out of individual moulds, topped with avo and black pepper, surrounded with salad leaves drizzled with a mustard vinaigrette*, and served with crisp rolls.

350 g English cucumber (that's 1 small or ½ large)

250 g smooth, low-fat cottage cheese (fat-free if preferred)

125 ml (½ cup) thick, low-fat Bulgarian yoghurt

2 ml (½ tsp) each sea salt and sugar

5 ml (1 tsp) Dijon mustard

22.5 ml (4½ tsp) gelatine

60 ml (¼ cup) cold water

30 ml (2 Tbsp) each finely chopped fresh parsley, chives and mint

125 ml (½ cup) thick cream, softly whipped

2 XL free-range egg whites, stiffly whisked

2 avocados, thinly segmented

milled black pepper for topping

Pare and grate the cucumber coarsely, and leave to drain in a colander – put a weight on the top to help squash out excess juice. Leave for about 30 minutes then, using your hands, squeeze as dry as possible. You should have 250 ml (1 cup). Whisk together the cottage cheese, yoghurt, salt, sugar and mustard. Sponge the gelatine in the water and dissolve over simmering water. Slowly dribble it into the cheese mixture, whisking all the time. Stir in the cucumber and herbs, then fold in the cream and egg whites. Check seasoning, then pour into six individual ramekins (rinsed for easy unmoulding) – they should be wide in diameter so that once unmoulded there will be a flat surface for the avo. Refrigerate for several hours until firm, or overnight. Just before serving, arrange the avocado in overlapping circles to cover the tops, and dust with a few grinds of pepper. **Serves 6.**

* Dress the salad leaves simply with olive oil and balsamic vinegar or verjuice, or make a **CREAMY MUSTARD VINAIGRETTE** by whizzing the following in a blender: 2 spring onions plus a bit of the tops, chopped; 1 clove garlic, chopped; 30 ml (2 Tbsp) *each* white balsamic vinegar and fresh lemon juice; 250 ml (1 cup) oil (at least half olive); 10 ml (2 tsp) whole-grain mustard; a small handful of parsley tufts; 5 ml (1 tsp) runny honey; 5 ml (1 tsp) dried tarragon; a pinch of salt. This makes a lovely, thick, pale green dressing. Refrigerate in a glass jar and shake before using.

Tomato Tartlets with Olives, Pesto & Pecorino

The popularity of tomato tarts never seems to wane and in this recipe they simply burst with Italian flavours and make super little cocktail snacks. A bit fiddly to prepare, but once you've got the bases made and the tomatoes grilled you can just line them up, stuff them and that's it. You'll need a small muffin tin for these, with the cups no more than 5 cm in base diameter and 2 cm deep. **The pastry will do 12.**

400 g puff pastry (buy it, and defrost in the fridge)

12 bella tomatoes (these are the size of a *very* large acorn)

olive oil, sea salt, sugar and dried oregano

walnut pesto* (or pesto of choice)

12 black olives, pitted and quartered

pecorino cheese, finely grated

pine nuts

* WALNUT PESTO

Place 30 g each basil and flat-leaf parsley (rinsed and thoroughly dried); 1 clove garlic, chopped; and 8 walnut halves in a processor fitted with the metal blade. Pulse finely and slowly dribble in about 100 ml (⅖ cup) olive oil. Remove and add a pinch of sea salt and 45 ml (3 Tbsp) finely grated pecorino cheese. Spoon into a glass jar, run a thin film of olive oil over the top and refrigerate. (You won't need all this for the tartlets, so save the rest for pasta.)

Roll out the pastry and cut out 12 circles, using a 7 cm cutter. Line the bases of the muffin tin cups with rounds of baking paper. Press a pastry circle firmly into each, prick the bases several times with a fork, and bake at 200 °C for 15–20 minutes or until risen, puffy and a light golden brown. Gently press down the centres to form a 'nest' and leave until cold before lifting out carefully. You can do these in advance and store in a cake tin overnight.

For the filling, slice the tomatoes in half but not right through – open out, place cut sides up in a flat oven dish or on a baking tray, sprinkle each with a few drops of olive oil and a pinch of salt, sugar and oregano, then grill until soft and juicy, beginning to shrivel, and smelling lovely. Nestle two halves in each pastry shell, top each with 2 ml (½ tsp) pesto and one quartered olive. Sprinkle with pecorino and gently press a few pine nuts into the top. Drizzle 2 ml (½ tsp) olive oil over each and place on a grill pan well below the griller, so that they will heat through gently without anything scorching. Remove when the nuts and pastry are lightly browned – be careful, they are soft and hot. Leave to cool a little before serving warm, or at room temperature. (They can also be reheated.)

Asparagus with a Choice of Dressings

Asparagus must surely be one of the world's most popular starters. Hot or cold, in soup, with mornay sauce, smothered in melted butter or with a delicious dressing for dipping, it's hard to go wrong. Buy the asparagus (slender and green, not thick and white) not more than one day in advance, and keep refrigerated. Before poaching, rinse well and snap off the bases, then place in a single layer in a wide-based, shallow saucepan with a little lightly salted boiling water and cook briefly, uncovered, until tender-crisp. Refresh under cold water to set the colour, drain on paper towels and serve with dressing of choice.

Quick Mustard Dressing

125 ml top-quality, off-the-shelf mayonnaise

125 ml low-fat Bulgarian yoghurt

15 ml (1 Tbsp) wholegrain mustard*

15 ml (1 Tbsp) pale, runny honey

1 ml (¼ tsp) dried tarragon, crushed

Gently mix all the ingredients with a spoon, turn into a glass jar, cover and refrigerate for a few hours at least.

* Wholegrain mustards differ in density – you may want a little more.
** Be very careful with uncooked egg yolks – keep the dressing refrigerated until the moment of serving, and if you wish to cut the richness of this dressing, gently fold in 1 part thick Bulgarian yoghurt to 3 parts dressing.

Orange-Mustard Dressing

1 whole XL free-range egg plus 1 yolk**

50 ml (⅕ cup) fresh orange juice

2 ml (½ tsp) finely grated orange rind

a pinch of sea salt

10 ml (2 tsp) pale, runny honey

250 ml (1 cup) oil

15 ml (1 Tbsp) wholegrain mustard

5 ml (1 tsp) brandy

Place the egg and yolk, orange juice and rind, salt and honey in a blender and blend until thoroughly combined. Very slowly, while blending, dribble in the oil. When all the oil has been used, the mixture should have a medium-thick consistency. Stir in the mustard and brandy, and refrigerate for several hours to thicken the mixture and to mature the flavour. To serve, arrange about six cooked and chilled asparagus spears on individual plates and spoon a generous dollop of dressing across the middle. **Serves 8–10.**

Chilled Spanspek Soup

It's slightly spicy, slightly sweet, most unusual and quite delicious. Make it in the hot summer months when spanspeks (sweet melons) are at their peak.

30 ml (2 Tbsp) oil
5 ml (1 tsp) butter
1 medium onion, chopped
2 leeks (white parts only), sliced
7 ml (1½ tsp) mild curry powder
2 ml (½ tsp) turmeric
a tiny knob of fresh root ginger, peeled and grated
1 stick cinnamon
1 whole star anise
1 small, ripe and bright spanspek, peeled and cubed (500 g prepared weight)
500 ml (2 cups) lightly seasoned chicken stock
250 ml (1 cup) milk
fresh lemon juice
thin, pouring cream and fresh coriander to garnish

Heat the oil and butter in a large saucepan, add the onion and leeks and allow to soften without browning. Add the spices and stir for a minute over low heat. Add the melon cubes, toss to mix, then add the stock. Cover and simmer over very low heat for about 15 minutes, until the melon cubes are very soft. Set aside to cool. Remove and discard the cinnamon and anise, then add the milk and puré in a blender until smooth – do this in batches. Check the seasoning and add a little lemon juice, just enough to sharpen the flavour. Pour into a fridge container, cover and refrigerate until icy cold, or up to 24 hours. To serve, pour into individual chilled soup cups, add a drizzle of cream to each – swirl into a cobweb, using a skewer – then scatter with a few fresh coriander leaves. **Serves 6.**

Aromatic Dhal Soup

A delicious mix of textures and spicy flavours mingle exuberantly in this ochre-coloured soup.
It's both easy and economical, and looks really inviting served in white soup bowls.

30 ml (2 Tbsp) each oil and butter
2 medium onions, chopped
3 cloves garlic, crushed
2 sticks cinnamon
5 ml (1 tsp) ground cumin
10 ml (2 tsp) each ground coriander
and turmeric
500 ml (2 cups) red lentils,
rinsed and drained
2 litres (8 cups) chicken stock
a little sea salt and sugar
30 ml (2 Tbsp) tomato paste
1 medium potato (125 g), peeled and
coarsely grated
thick Bulgarian yoghurt, garam masala
and fresh coriander leaves to garnish

Heat the oil and butter in a large saucepan. Add the onions and garlic and, when softening, add the spices. Allow them to sizzle for a minute or two over low heat, adding a dash of water if necessary to prevent scorching. Add the remaining ingredients, except the garnish, bring to the boil, then cover and simmer gently, stirring occasionally, for about 25 minutes or until the lentils and potato are soft and the ingredients have cooked almost to a puré. Stir vigorously to combine and, if too thick, add a little more stock. Check seasoning, remove and discard the cinnamon, and spoon the soup into warmed bowls. Top each serving with a dollop of yoghurt, sprinkle with garam masala, and surround with a few coriander leaves. **Serves 8–10.**

Butternut, Butter Bean, Coconut & Basmati Soup

Surprising ingredients, lots of spices, unexpected textures and the brightest colour all combine to make this one really special. It's *quite* different from the usual run of soups, and although the list of ingredients might look intimidating, don't be fazed because it's really easy, amazingly good, and you *definitely* won't need a main course after this meal-in-one.

cooked yellow basmati rice

30 ml (2 Tbsp) oil

1 large onion, finely chopped

1 large butternut, peeled and cut into small dice (600 g prepared weight)

300 g carrots, diced

7 ml (1½ tsp) ground cumin

5 ml (1 tsp) ground coriander

4 cm piece fresh root ginger, peeled and coarsely grated

2 stalks lemon grass, white parts only, bruised (optional)

1 x 400 ml can coconut milk (regular or lite)

250 ml (1 cup) chicken stock

a little sea salt

1 x 400 g can butter beans, drained and rinsed

a large handful of fresh coriander leaves

fresh lemon juice

garam masala

naan bread to serve

Start with the basmati rice – for this recipe, cook 125 ml (½ cup) as usual, adding 1 ml (¼ tsp) turmeric to the cooking water. When done, cover and leave. You can even re-heat it if working ahead – add a little water, heat gently, and loosen with a fork. For the soup, heat the oil in a very large saucepan, sauté the onion until golden (adding a pinch of sugar helps, as there is no butter to add a little colour), then add the vegetables and spices and toss until aromatic. Add the lemon grass, if using, the coconut milk, stock and salt. Cover and simmer until the vegetables are soft – about 45 minutes. If the vegetables are still a bit chunky, remove the lemon grass and then use a potato masher to reduce the veg – not too much, leave some texture. Add the beans and coriander and heat through, then add just enough lemon juice to sharpen the taste. If the soup seems too thick, add a little more stock. Ladle into deep, heated soup bowls. Gently place a large spoonful of rice in the centre (you probably won't need all the rice). Dust with garam masala, and serve with hot naan bread. **Serves 4 hugely and, if doubling up, use a really enormous saucepan.**

Minted Cucumber & Yoghurt Soup with Walnuts

A *thoroughly* unusual soup, pale and creamy and crunchy all at the same time. In fact, it might cause a bit of a *skrik* at the first sip, because it's so different from chilled, creamy soups. But it's really good, and if you're looking for something *quite* different and refreshing with which to start off a meal on a hot summer's evening, this one could hit just the right spot.

500 g English cucumber
375 ml (1½ cups) plain, stirred Bulgarian yoghurt (not thick yoghurt)
1 small clove garlic, chopped
1 slim spring onion, chopped
125 ml (½ cup) thin cream
8 small to medium fresh mint leaves (avoid the large older ones)
pinch of sea salt, and sugar to taste
extra cucumber cubes and chopped walnuts to garnish

Pare the cucumber, slice into long strips, flick out all the seeds, then cut into small cubes. You should have 400 g. Poach in a little salted water over low heat – use a wide-based frying pan so that the cubes can be spread out – until soft and translucent. Watch that the water doesn't boil away, adding a little more if it looks dry before the cucumber is soft. When done, drain if necessary, then puré in a blender with the yoghurt, garlic, spring onion, cream and mint – the mixture should be smooth, creamy and faintly flecked with green. Before removing from the blender, taste – it will need a little sugar and perhaps a pinch of salt or another mint leaf or two. Chill overnight in a glass container, loosely covered. Before serving, check seasoning – if the flavour is too tart, stir in a little runny honey – it makes all the difference. Into each small chilled soup cup place 30 ml (2 Tbsp) cucumber cubes (prepared as above), pour in some soup, scatter with walnuts, and serve.
Serves 4–5 and is easily doubled.

Quick Gazpacho with Whipped Basil Cream

A speedy version of the popular Spanish summer soup, using a method which, although not traditional, puts it within reach of the busiest cook. Normally, gazpacho is served with chopped salad ingredients and croûtons – but a surprising topping of savoury cream gives the old favourite a new look and a smoother flavour.

2 x 2 cm thick slices crustless bread

600 g ripe tomatoes, peeled, seeded and chopped

1 large English cucumber, pared, seeded and chopped

1 fat clove garlic, chopped

1 large leek (white part only), chopped

400 ml (1⅗ cups) tomato juice (not tomato cocktail)

5 ml (1 tsp) each sea salt and sugar

15 ml (1 Tbsp) red wine vinegar

30 ml (2 Tbsp) olive oil

1 red pepper, seeded, ribs removed, and chopped

BASIL CREAM

125 ml (½ cup) fresh cream

about 10 fresh basil leaves, torn

a pinch each of salt and paprika

Soak the bread briefly in a little water and squeeze dry, then mix with the remaining ingredients in a large bowl. Spoon into a blender and puré in batches, until almost smooth. Do not expect a velvety result – although the vegetables should be completely pulped, the mixture will appear mushy and rather thick. This is correct, as gazpacho is served over ice cubes, which thin it down a little. Turn into a fridge container and chill. The soup should be served after about 2 hours, but will hold for longer if necessary.

For the basil cream, whisk together all the ingredients until fairly thick, then chill until needed.

Give the soup a good stir before serving, and check seasoning. Pour into chilled bowls over a cube or two of ice, and top each serving with a dollop of basil cream – either left in a big blob, or swirled into a cobweb. **Serves 8.**

Bean, Pasta & Vegetable Soup

Using a can of beans instead of soaking and cooking haricots is a clever short cut, and means that in just one hour you can have a chunky, really substantial meal-in-a-soup at very little cost. A teaspoon of pesto swirled into each serving adds a marvellous zip to the flavour, but if you don't have pesto, pass freshly grated pecorino for sprinkling, a loaf of crusty bread and a carafe of red wine. Perfect for a wintry Sunday supper, and no main course needed after this nourishing soup.

30 ml (2 Tbsp) oil
2 onions, chopped
2 cloves garlic, crushed
3–4 carrots, diced
3 sticks celery, plus some leaves, sliced
2 litres (8 cups) chicken or vegetable stock
125 ml (½ cup) tomato puré
a handful of flat-leaf parsley, chopped
about 5 ml (1 tsp) sea salt
a large pinch of sugar
1 x 420 g can baked beans in tomato sauce
250 ml (1 cup) elbow macaroni
750 ml (3 cups) finely shredded spinach leaves (ribs removed)
2 ml (½ tsp) dried oregano

Heat the oil in a large saucepan, add the onions and garlic and soften without browning. Add the carrots and celery and stir-fry briefly. Add the stock, tomato puré, parsley and seasoning. Cover and simmer gently for about 25 minutes, until the vegetables are cooked. Add the remaining ingredients, return to the boil, then cover and simmer over low heat for 30 minutes, stirring occasionally to prevent sticking – you might have to add a little extra stock. Check seasoning, ladle into deep, warmed soup bowls, and garnish each serving as suggested above. **Serves 8.**

Spicy Pumpkin & Apple Soup

Despite the unsophisticated ingredients, this soup is amazingly good with its subtle mix of spices and brilliant colour. Be sure to use a bright orange, firm-fleshed pumpkin – if I buy a whole pumpkin and find, when sliced, that I am not altogether happy about the colour or texture, I use half butternut and half pumpkin, but I still call it pumpkin soup. A rose by any other name …

30 ml (2 Tbsp) oil
10 ml (2 tsp) butter
1 large onion, chopped
500 g pumpkin, peeled and cubed (prepared weight)
1 medium potato, peeled and cubed
2 medium dessert apples, peeled and sliced
5 ml (1 tsp) mild curry powder
2 ml (½ tsp) turmeric
2 ml (½ tsp) ground cinnamon
1 medium knob fresh root ginger, peeled and grated – about 10 ml (2 tsp)
750 ml (3 cups) chicken or vegetable stock
a little sea salt
2 bay leaves
125–200 ml (½–⅞ cup) milk
fresh lemon juice
fresh coriander leaves to garnish

Heat the oil and butter in a large saucepan, add the onion and, when soft and golden, add the pumpkin, potato, apples and spices and toss together over low heat for about 2 minutes, until coated and aromatic. Add the stock, salt and bay leaves, bring to the boil, then cover and simmer over very low heat until the vegetables are soft – about 25 minutes. Cool to lukewarm, remove the bay leaves and puré in a blender, in batches, until absolutely smooth. Reheat, adding just enough milk to achieve a medium-thick consistency – the soup should be velvety and creamy even though there's no cream in it. Check the seasoning, and if the flavour needs sharpening add a squeeze of fresh lemon juice. Ladle into soup bowls and top each serving with a few coriander leaves. **Serves 6.**

Smoked Salmon & Green Bean Salad

Because smoked salmon is expensive, it's a good idea to pad it out with other ingredients to make it go further. If you choose these ingredients carefully the result will be creative, rather than mean. In the following starter salad the addition of anchovies and slim-as-a-bridge-pencil green beans do the trick, and the result is an unusual combination, topped with just a flutter of salmon and served with lightly buttered rye bread. Nevertheless, it is a special-occasion and not a budget salad.

400 g very slim green beans, trimmed and halved diagonally OR
300 g green beans and 200 g button mushrooms, wiped and thinly sliced
1 large onion, sliced into thin rings
2 ml (½ tsp) dried dill
1 large red or yellow pepper, seeded, ribs removed, and julienned
120–160 g smoked salmon, rolled and thinly shredded
sour cream, milled black pepper and lemon slices to garnish

DRESSING
100 ml (⅖ cup) oil
1 x 50 g can anchovy fillets, drained and briefly soaked in milk, then drained again
a few tufts of parsley
30 ml (2 Tbsp) fresh lemon juice
a pinch of sugar

Cook the beans, mushrooms (if using), onion and dill in a little unsalted water in a large frying pan until the beans are tender and still bright green – don't cover the pan completely, keep the lid tilted. While this is happening, make the dressing by placing the oil, *half* the anchovies and the rest of the ingredients in a blender and blend until smooth. When the beans are ready, drain (but do not refresh), place in a bowl, pour the dressing over, fork in the red or yellow pepper, cool, then cover and chill for 3–4 hours. Just before serving, toss in the remaining anchovies, chopped, and arrange on individual small plates. Top with the salmon, a dollop of sour cream, and a dusting of pepper, and place a slice of lemon on the side. Serve with rye bread. **Makes 6 small servings.**

Salad with Rosemary Pears & Blue Cheese Dressing

A salad always gets a meal off to a good start, but, to qualify as a starter, it *has* to be different from the usual tossed green salad. This one is. A combination of leafy greens with roasted peppers, walnuts and subtly perfumed pears, it looks lovely piled onto a large platter*, allowing diners to help themselves. Easy to prepare in advance, and the quantities for leafy ingredients are adaptable, depending on the number of diners; the pears will slot into a salad for four to six, so double up for a jumbo salad; the dressing, served separately, will do for about 10 servings.

BASE SALAD

A mixture of baby spinach, rocket, watercress and lettuce leaves.

PEPPERS

2 large red peppers, halved, seeds and ribs removed, opened out flat and grilled until blistered and blackened. Cover with a damp towel, remove skin and slice into strips.

PEARS

Peel and halve 3 large, not-quite-ripe pears, e.g. Packham's. Place in a wide pan, rounded sides up, sprinkle each half with a pinch of sugar and 5 ml (1 tsp) lemon juice, add 250 ml (1 cup) water and 2 x 10 cm sprigs rosemary, bring to the boil, then reduce the heat and simmer, covered, until *just* tender – test by pricking with a skewer. Leave to cool uncovered (the perfume is a knock-out), then remove the pears with a slotted spoon and refrigerate. Before serving, remove pips and cores and slice into segments.

TOPPING

Coarsely chopped walnuts or pecan nuts.

DRESSING

250 ml (1 cup) oil (half olive, half canola or sunflower); 90 ml (6 Tbsp) fresh lemon juice; 60 g blue cheese, crumbled (or more to taste); 5 ml (1 tsp) Worcestershire sauce; 1 small clove garlic, chopped; a few tufts of parsley; 2 spring onions, chopped; a little trickle of honey. Place in a blender and blend until creamy. Pour into a jug or jar, refrigerate, and shake or whisk just before serving. Optional: for a milder, creamier dressing, stir in up to 125 ml (½ cup) thick plain yoghurt.

ACCOMPANIMENT

Baguette slices, brushed with olive oil, lightly toasted and rubbed with a cut clove of garlic.

* Use a large, shallow platter in order to show off the different ingredients and colours before they all get mixed up.

Flora

Corriebush was a neat little town.

'Shipshape is how we describe it,' the women would inform visitors when taking them round to show off the sights.

And they certainly had reason to feel proud, for the houses were regularly white-washed, or painted in pastel shades; hedges always clipped as straight as arrows; and every garden meticulously designed – with flowers blooming in circular beds, and bird-baths or jolly gnomes planted neatly in the centres. Each front gate displayed a street number in shiny, polished brass, and many had name-plaques: *Ons Huisie*, 'Rest-Awhile,' or a combination of the owners' first names – like Charlie and Nellie, who called their house 'Charnel.'

The council regularly trimmed all the trees lining the pavements, except for the jacarandas, because everyone loved the purple blooms that floated down and carpeted the streets. There were no litter bins, because nobody littered. It was a neat town.

There was only one house in the whole of Corriebush that was totally neglected. The women were discussing it over tea on Lily's stoep.

'A dreadful sore eye.'

'*Eye-sore*, Sophia.'

'Eye-sore. It gives the town a bad name.'

'Lowers the tone of the place.'

'I can't understand why somebody doesn't buy it. There's lots of potential there, they could do it up very nicely.'

'I wonder who built it in the first place?'

'Servaas says it was a convict who escaped from England on a ship, but then he died, and now it's haunted.'

'*Ag*, Servaas and his nonsense.'

Certainly the house did look spooky, standing lonely and scarred in the middle of a forest of weeds and twisted trees. The shutters hung limply, whipped loose by years of shrill winter winds, while a century of sun had raked the plaster from the bleached, pitted walls. The windows stared blindly, all shattered and empty, with only a jagged pane here and there reflecting glints of blue sky. It was a dead house.

And then one day, a lorry rumbled down the main street, a huge lorry loaded with bricks, bags of cement and wooden beams. With a loud grinding of gears and a great deal of hooting and bumping, it climbed the pavement before turning sharply into Marigold Avenue, where it grumbled to a stop outside the old house.

No sooner had the driver pulled up the brake when Lily was there. Amelia was not far behind, untying her apron as she rounded the corner, followed by Anna and Sophia and Nellie and Maria. But Daleen – Corriebush's estate agent – had beaten them to it, and was standing, notebook in hand, looking important.

'What's going on here Daleen? Have you sold it at last? You didn't tell us anything!'

Daleen took some time to answer, first chatting to the driver, then directing him, waving her arm this way and that. 'Swing this way! No, no, sharp left. That's it. Now reverse. Slowly, slowly, that's right, try revving a little bit now. There you go! Brilliant!'

'DALEEN?'

'Just a minute Lily. I'll tell you everything later, when I've supervised the delivery. It's a tricky job, you know, and I'm in charge. Cash client. A V.I.P.'

The lorry finally made it into the pot-holed driveway, coming to rest in a fog of dust and engine fumes. When everything had been dumped, Daleen sat down on a broken log.

'It's a rich lady from the coast. She made enquiries, top secret you know, and I posted her all the details and she sent an architect to draw up plans for renovation. Then she bought it on the spot – no, I'm a professional and I cannot disclose the sum. That wouldn't be ethical, and if I'm anything, I'm ethical. The lady said she was buying it on behalf of a good friend, and she thought it would suit her perfectly.'

'Well, that's very nice,' said Sophia, swatting the air with her hands. 'But if that driver doesn't get himself fitted with a new exhaust pipe I'm not coming again.'

Nevertheless, she joined the others as they eagerly watched the house mushroom into life: sash windows, two gables, a teak front door and a verandah all the way round with a view over the town and straight onto the mountain. The garden was cleared and planted with calendulas and nasturtiums, which surrounded a fishpond with a mermaid in the middle. After three months the job was complete. And then the furniture arrived.

'Antique stuff,' Amelia told Daniel, who knew about furniture.

'A yellowwood dining table, two Paul Kruger chairs, a stinkwood *riempie* bench for the verandah, a four-poster bed, a French armoire and a *linnekas* and ...'

'Enough. There's a story there. Suddenly a woman no-one has ever heard of, a total stranger with a lot of money, buys a dilapidated house in Corriebush, fixes it up, then dispatches a friend to come and live in it. Strange. Very strange. Tell Lily to go and find out more.'

Flora Lategan arrived on Wednesday of the following week, and the women knew immediately because they had been keeping a daily watch. On the Tuesday the house was, as Nellie said, up and running but as quiet as a mouse, and then on the Wednesday evening – right out of the blue – there was a woman sitting on the stinkwood bench on the front verandah.

'We must call on her,' Lily told them, when they had gathered in her kitchen after supper. 'Tomorrow. With a few eats and maybe one of those fancy cards. "Wishing You Bunches of Happiness In Your New Home". Something like that.'

'I'll bake scones,' said Nellie.

'I'll take the jam,' said Amelia.

'Pumpkin fritters for me,' said Sophia.

And so they arrived all together the next morning, lifting the new brass knocker on the front door, quite breathless with the joy of it all, for welcoming strangers to Corriebush was such a pleasure.

The woman who answered their knock was, they saw immediately, one of their own. Middle-aged and smiling. Kind, gentle face. Hair in a bun. 'Goodness gracious me!' she exclaimed, clapping her hands. 'Isn't this a surprise! Come in, come in!' And she put out her hand. 'Flora Lategan from up the coast, near Plet. But just call me Florrie. Everyone does. Sometimes even Floribunda. I don't mind.'

One by one they shook her hand and introduced themselves.

'Well now, do sit down. Where shall we go? The dining room is a bit dusty still, so maybe the kitchen is the place, if you ladies don't mind?' They were delighted, other people's kitchens were always of great interest to them. Surprisingly, it turned out to be an old-fashioned sort of kitchen. Large deal table, an Aga stove, open wooden dresser hung with china cups. 'I wanted a kitchen just like Martha's,' said Flora. 'To remind me of her always.'

'Quite so,' they nodded, not understanding any of it.

'Such a lovely lady,' Flora went on. 'All this that you see here is thanks to Martha.'

'How very kind,' they agreed.

'It's not every day that somebody gives one a house.'

'With furniture and everything.'

'Is Martha your rich aunt, then?'

'*Ag*, I'm so stupid. Of course you don't know Martha. But let me first pour the tea and butter these delicious scones you brought, and then we can 'chew the fat' as they say.'

Sophia couldn't wait. 'Never mind the fat, Florrie. We've all got enough of that. We're just longing to know who you are. I mean, we like you very much and all that, but we don't know anything about anything. And so on,' she finished, losing her thread completely.

Anna came to the rescue.

'What is your trade, Florrie?'

'She means profession,' Lily quickly corrected her.

'I'm a district nurse,' Florrie answered. 'You know, I go round with my medical kit and visit sick people in their homes.'

'And then?' Sophia was back again, wanting to know.

'Well, I try to help them, and sometimes my patients become my friends. It goes like that with district nurses.'

'And then?'

Flora realised there was no stopping Sophia. She would simply have to begin at the beginning. 'Fill your cups,' she told them. So they poured quickly, and then sat back eagerly, waiting.

'It all started in Plettenberg Bay. My agency sent me there, and one of my patients was a lady called Martha Foster. She lived alone, in a big house overlooking the bay. She kept to herself, seldom leaving the house, spending most of her time sitting on a bench in her garden looking out to sea.'

'And so?'

'Before my first visit I asked the people in the village about her. It always helps if you have a little background about your patients before you start. And they told me her story.'

Immediately the women fell silent. This was what they loved best, and the very air in the kitchen rippled with anticipation. Their tea grew cold, the scones lay crumbled, half-eaten.

'Martha Foster was a lovely girl. Tall and slender with gypsy-dark eyes and long, wavy black hair. Sometimes she drew it back and tied it with a red ribbon, but usually it swung free and shining, the colour of midnight, and when she walked in the wind it wrapped round her like a cloak. She and Edward Bellamy made a striking pair and the villagers always turned to look as they passed, for he was as fair as she was dark, and they were young and in love.

'*Ag siestog,*' said Sophia.

'The wedding was set to coincide with Martha's eighteenth birthday and, once the engagement had been announced, the small community hummed with excitement. This, everyone knew, was to be a memorable wedding because Martha Foster was no ordinary village girl. She had been only four years old when her parents had been drowned in a shipwreck. Sailing to England, the *Crusader* had run aground in a storm near Algoa Bay, and Martha's guardian had brought her to live with her great-aunt Dora.'

The women were leaning forward now, elbows on the table, eyes fixed on Flora. Romantic stories were their favourites.

'Dora Foster was an artist, a spinster who had settled in a small cottage in the village, because painting seascapes was her speciality. Finding that she was suddenly in charge of a four-year-old child came as a big shock. She wasn't at all sure how to handle the little girl, so she simply sent her off each morning to spend her days with the other village children. And so Martha grew up barefoot and free, a child of the wind and the water just like the rest of them.

'Until the day Aunt Dora told her about the money.'

'The *money*?'

'Now *there's* a thing.'

'I *knew* there was a twist coming.'

Florrie ignored the interruptions.

'It was the morning of Martha's tenth birthday. Aunt Dora called her to come to her studio – a small, dusty room, slanted with sunlight and splashed with easels and paint. Stepping back from the canvas on which she was working, she cocked her head to one side and said, 'You should know, child, that on your eighteenth birthday you will inherit the Foster fortune.' That was all. The old lady dipped her brush into the purple paint-water and, head, still on one side, returned to her easel.

'The villagers said a few of them had been listening at the open window while Dora was speaking, and that Martha had stood quite still in a pool of sunlight. The child was probably having a wonderful vision of bags and bags full of gold coins. Then she skipped

out of the room and down the sandy track to tell her friends. The children told their parents, and the news rippled through the village. The child was an heiress. She would be a very rich lady. 'But whom,' they asked, 'will the poor little thing marry?'

'*Ag* shame.' Sophia could not help herself.

'Not one of their sons, they decided sadly. Not a mere fisherman's son. No, her groom would have to be a man from the city, or even a foreign country, not a poor fisherman's son. And from that day Martha was set apart. Not unkindly; the children still played with her as they had always done, but she gradually became aware that she was no longer one of them. The fact of the matter was that she was an heiress with a destiny far beyond that of the average village child.'

'Florrie does use big words,' whispered Nellie.

'Shhh. She's not a district nurse for nothing.'

'They watched as Martha grew from a sunburnt, leggy waif to a slender beauty. They watched while the other girls of her age were pairing off with boys, and Martha was never approached. The local lads were friendly enough, helped carry her school books and so on – but they never kissed her round corners the way they kissed the other girls. They knew her story. She was too grand for them. And Martha began to feel really lonely and bewildered. Until the day – the memorable day – that Edward Bellamy arrived in the village.

'It was a crisp, clear morning in the middle of winter, when the sand squeaked cold underfoot, and the waves – navy blue, winter waves – splintered on the beach like ice on

stone. The men were out in their boats on the bay, their wives busy mending their nets, spread out like giant cobwebs on the silky sand. Striding along the water's edge came a barefoot and bronzed young man, kitbag in hand, long blonde hair down to his shoulders. Edward was a sailor. No-one knew where he had come from, but he turned up that winter's day and before the sun had set in the evening all the women were clucking with excitement. Here was a stranger, a romantic and handsome stranger, and there was Martha, as ripe and ready to be picked as the juicy pomegranates that grew in every garden – perhaps, perhaps at last …

'Ooh, now I've got gooseflesh,' said Anna, wrapping her arms round her shoulders.

'Edward had a pack of adventure stories to tell. Day after day he would sit on the beach, a far-away look in his deep blue eyes, and spin tales about elephants in Ceylon and giant snakes in South America; of glistening white icebergs and massive killer whales; of Oriental silks and precious jewels and of storms at sea when the waves rose up like dark glass mountains.

'The simple village folk listened in wide-eyed disbelief. The children leapt with questions. They asked to hear the stories over and over again, and so the days became weeks, and the weeks became months, and by the time Edward had been accepted and assigned a regular place on a fishing boat, he and Martha were engaged. The villagers were overjoyed.

'As soon as the wedding date had been set and the banns drawn up, they started improving the little church for the occasion, repairing the roof, hammering together new pews. At last this wedding – this wonderfully romantic wedding – would perfectly complete the story of Martha.

'But even as they sawed and planed and plastered, even as Martha put the finishing touches to her wedding dress and Aunt Dora started painting her portrait, Edward was desperately trying to explain to her that he needed to go on just one more voyage. He was a sailor, and he loved the sea as much as he loved her. He wasn't ready yet, he said, to settle down as a fisherman. 'Please, please try to understand,' he pleaded over and over. 'I have to go just *once* more. A few months – and then I'll be back forever. We'll be married, and I'll build you a house right on the beach.'

'*Ag* no,' interrupted Lily. 'I just *knew* he was going to put a spanner in the works. It always happens.'

'Well, on the day that Edward sailed for Spain, Martha stood on the shore until the sea lay empty; until the little ship with its cluster of taut, white sails had edged round

The Point and slowly dipped below the horizon. And then, anxiously twisting her hair into a coil as she walked, she returned to the village and to Aunt Dora's little whitewashed cottage – to wait.

'Each day Martha went down to the water's edge and looked out to sea. Through the dazzling blue summers and the wild, tossing winters she waited, while her gaiety grew old and died. The villagers stood by mutely, watching in dismay as their romantic dream faded. And when eventually the first streaks of grey threaded her long black hair, Martha used some of her inheritance to build the house on the cliff. For Edward.

'And there she waited – in the house on the cliff – the great white house that shimmered in the heat of the summers, shuddered in the winds of winter, and glowed gently at night with the light of a candle burning brightly in a window, like a beacon. Her lovely face became sad and lined; her graceful figure became thinner and wasted. And still she waited.'

Now Florrie stopped to take a sip of her cold tea. Some of the women had tears in their eyes. They clucked their tongues, shook their heads, completely overcome by the thought of Martha's heartache.

'Now this,' continued Flora, 'was when the agency sent me to Plettenberg Bay, and one of the patients on my list was Martha. She had had a bad fall and injured her knee and I was to go and see what could be done.

'When I first knocked at the door, there was no response. Then I heard a soft voice asking "Who is it?". I turned the knob and, finding it unlocked, went inside. Martha was sitting in an old armchair, knitting. She looked quite frail, but her face was still lovely, and her hair carefully swept up. She looked at me with those dark eyes and said nothing. I examined her leg – it was only badly bruised – so I bandaged it, and offered to make her some tea. She was so grateful, and I started visiting her every day, cooking a hot meal, and staying for a chat. Soon she was no longer just a patient, we became friends.

'Shame. She must have been so lonely until you came, sitting in that big empty house all alone.'

'No, no, it was beautifully furnished. Comfortable sofas everywhere and paintings on the walls – but she always sat in the same chair next to the same little table. On it stood

a framed photograph of a young blonde sailor. She did not know that I knew her story, and I never referred to it. But one day an incredible thing happened.'

Just then there was a knock at Flora's front door. It was Harry the postman, and while she left the kitchen to receive her post, the women sat like statues, speechless for once, unable to anticipate the next chapter.

'What happened,' Florrie resumed, sitting down, 'was that one day a sailor, a young blonde sailor, with his kitbag over his shoulder, came bounding up the old steps and hammered on the front door.

I saw him, through the window. Of course I answered his knock, and opened the door. And there on the doorstep stood the young man in the photograph.'

'*Ag* no Florrie! That's impossible!' the women gasped. 'Now you're telling stories. How could it be?'

Flora smiled. 'The young Edward Bellamy had none of his Spanish mother's dark beauty; he was big and blonde like his father. He had come to visit Martha, he said, because his father had told him all about her after his mother had died. "My father is quite an old man now, living in Barcelona. It was here that he met my mother when his ship was in port for a few weeks. My mother was very beautiful, and he says he completely lost his heart. But Father never forgot his first love. And he said if my travels should ever bring me to this place, that I should please visit her and tell her he would always remember her, and to give her his fondest wishes." And he moved forward, as though to step inside.

'Quick as a wink I jammed my foot into the doorway. And I told him, I said, "Listen here, young man! If you think you're going to just march in here and upset Martha Foster you'd better think again. No, no, NO! I have news for you. You're going straight back to your Spain, and you're going to fetch your father. You're going to bring him here with you – and then – and only then will I let you into this house."

'Well, young Edward Bellamy just stood there and looked at me for a long time. I think he was shocked. But he stood there for so long that eventually I stood aside and he saw past me to where Martha was sitting, the sun was shining on her face and hair and she was looking out of the window at the sea. I think that was when he made up his mind.

'It wasn't more than three months later that the two of them walked up the steps together. Martha and I were playing a game of cards when I glanced up and saw them coming. I waited for them to knock. 'I wonder who that can be,' she said. 'If it's the baker, tell him two loaves, please.'

'Well, I rushed. Flung the door open and stood aside, and in they walked. First the father, and then the son.'

'And then?' asked Sophia, wringing her hands.

'*Ag* ladies, don't ask me to describe what passed between those two people in that emotional moment. I just turned and looked the other way, both the son and I. Then we walked into the garden and stayed there, looking at the sea for a long time, before going back inside.'

'I can't stand it,' wailed Amelia. 'What did they do? Did they speak? Did they cry? Hold hands?'

Flora shrugged. 'Who's to know? But what I can tell you is that the two old people live there together now. The parson read a marriage service and she wears a ring, and every day they walk together on the beach, and the villagers – those who still remember them – smile and wave as they pass.'

'Oh my, oh goodness me, *what* a story! It's just like a book!'

'It makes me quite sad, it's so lovely, I mean that she got him after all.'

'But I still don't know how you come to be in Corriebush.' Sophia tapped the table-top with one finger. 'Here. How do you come to be here?'

'Listen, then. Martha found out that I was the one who had arranged their meeting. Edward told her. She insisted on giving me a huge amount of money and when I refused to take it she took matters into her own

hands. She and Edward consulted estate agents, chose an architect, and had this house re-built for me; they even had it furnished with these lovely pieces. But she instructed the architect to keep the kitchen old-looking because we had had so many happy meals in hers, and she wanted me to remember.'

'What an angel.'

'And she chose Corriebush because she knew I had grown up in the Karoo and always longed to return.'

'So how did she tell you? I mean, one can't wrap up a house like other presents!

'She asked me to come to supper one evening, she and Edward, and they handed me the title deeds. I cried then.'

'Shame, Florrie.'

'You see, I had worked all my life, and I had very little money, and she gave me my freedom. I can never thank her enough. I'll visit them often, of course, Martha and Edward. Yes, I'll keep an eye on them, take them photographs of the house, and rusks and venison and figs and other Corriebush things. But this is my home now.'

'Oh yes,' they repeated, all misty-eyed. 'This is your home now.'

Sophia had the last word. '*Ag* what a beautiful story, Florrie. Just like a fairy tale.'

And for once she had got it right.

Mains

Salmon with Stir-fried Vegetables

If you dislike frying fish, try this one. It's a super, stove-top dish, delicately touched with Oriental seasonings that don't intrude on the fine flavour of Cape salmon, but it's also good with the old faithful – hake. If you prepare the vegetables in advance, it does not take much standing over the stove, and it's light and healthy. The one imperative: a very large pan – 28 x 6 cm is perfect.

45 ml (3 Tbsp) oil

5 ml (1 tsp) dark sesame oil

a bunch of spring onions or a few baby leeks, chopped

a small knob of fresh root ginger, peeled and coarsely grated

3 medium carrots, julienned

180 g slender green beans, trimmed and diagonally sliced

½ English cucumber (250 g), pared and julienned (seeds discarded)

125 g button mushrooms, wiped, sliced

4 Cape salmon fillets (550–600 g total weight) (skin removed)

sea salt and milled black pepper

toasted almond flakes to garnish

SAUCE

250 ml (1 cup) fish or chicken stock

30 ml (2 Tbsp) cornflour

about 30 ml (2 Tbsp) soy sauce (depending on the brand)

5 ml (1 tsp) honey

2–5 ml (½–1 tsp) finely grated lemon rind

Heat the oils in that large pan and stir-fry the spring onions or leeks, ginger, carrots and beans until softening but still crunchy. (You could also cover the pan and let them steam over a low heat.) Add the cucumber and mushrooms, and toss until wilting. Stir together all the ingredients for the sauce, add to the pan and, when bubbling and thickened, reduce the heat to very low and arrange the lightly seasoned fish on top of the vegetables. Cover and allow to simmer very gently for 10–12 minutes or until the fish is just cooked through. Using a slotted spoon, carefully transfer the fillets to a warmed serving platter, best side up, sprinkle with almonds and spoon the saucy vegetables alongside. **Serves 4.**

Roasted Cape Salmon with Butter & Herbs

An amazingly effortless fish dish – no frying, no turning, no grilling. No fishy haze in the kitchen. No garnishing. It's astonishing that it can turn out so well when almost all that is required of the cook is the making of the butter – that, and having in hand a perfect piece of thick, skinned salmon fillet, weighing 500 g. The dill and tarragon used in this recipe are dried, because all too often they are unobtainable fresh – either they're out of season, or the supermarket is fresh out. But dried herbs, freshly bought, make an excellent butter, and the flavour of this dish is lovely.

60 ml (4 Tbsp) soft butter
1 ml (¼ tsp) dried dill
1 ml (¼ tsp) dried tarragon
15 ml (1 Tbsp) finely snipped chives
15 ml (1 Tbsp) finely chopped parsley
2 ml (½ tsp) finely grated lemon rind
500 g skinless salmon fillet in one piece of even thickness
60 ml (¼ cup) white wine (Sauvignon Blanc is a good choice)
sea salt

First cream the butter with the herbs and lemon rind, mixing well. Roll into a sausage-shape, wrap and refrigerate for about 1 hour, or until firm enough to slice. To bake, place the fish in a baking dish – not a big one – it should fit fairly snugly with a bit of room to spare for the juices. Pour the wine in at the side and season the fish lightly. Slice the butter into 6 coins and place them on top of the fish in two rows of three. Roast at 200 C for 15 minutes, then remove from the oven and spread any blobs of butter that have not melted, over the fish, giving it a green coating. Give a quick baste with the winey juices and return to the oven for 5 minutes, or until the fish is just cooked through. To serve, slice the fish into four and spoon some juices over each serving. Oven-roasted potato wedges go well with this – simply scrub and cube potatoes, season, roll in olive oil and place in the hot oven about 30 minutes before the fish. For veg, a stir-fry is great: green beans, button mushrooms, julienned baby marrows and carrots, chopped leeks – all good. **This fish dish will serve 4, and is easily doubled.**

Spicy Stove-top Fish Curry

The Karoo might teem with game and lamb and beef, but there's no fish in the veld. Sometimes there isn't any at my nearest city fish market either. Fresh out of fresh. I'm talking hake here, which is good for a curry – and so this recipe uses frozen, and very satisfying it is too, in a thick, bright, fairly hot sauce. Good with basmati rice (add a touch of turmeric when cooking) and serve with yoghurt and cucumber.

45 ml (3 Tbsp) oil and a pat of butter

1 large onion, chopped

1 red chilli, seeded and chopped

2 cloves garlic, crushed

20 ml (4 tsp) curry powder

5 ml (1 tsp) ground cumin

2 ml (½ tsp) ground fennel

250 ml (1 cup) fish or chicken stock

1 x 400 g can tomatoes

about 250 g baby marrows, pared and diced (200 g prepared weight)

30 ml (2 Tbsp) chutney

2 bay leaves

5 ml (1 tsp) tomato paste

sugar to taste

500 g skinned and filleted frozen hake portions

seasoned flour

fresh coriander leaves

Heat the oil and butter in a *very* large frying pan, add the onion, chilli and garlic and, when softening, add the spices, stirring for a few seconds over low heat. Place *half* the stock, the tomatoes plus juice and the baby marrows in a blender and pulse briefly to chop and mix to a chunky consistency. Add to the pan, together with the chutney, bay leaves, tomato paste and a little sugar to offset the tart tomatoes. (The mixture will look very 'seedy' at this stage, but don't worry, it will smooth out to create a thick and succulent sauce.) Cover and simmer very gently for about 20 minutes to concentrate the flavour. Dust the fish lightly with seasoned flour, shaking off any excess, and slide into the sauce – at this stage it will be very dense, so add the remaining 125 ml (½ cup) stock – you may even need a little more. Keeping the heat low, cover and simmer until the fish is cooked right through – turn once, carefully. The cooking time depends on the size of your pan and the thickness of the fillets. Remove the bay leaves, and sprinkle with fresh coriander. **Serves 4.**

Roasted Fish, Italian-style

I've never eaten this dish in Italy and possibly the Italians haven't either, but it's as good a name as any for fish teamed up with Mediterranean ingredients. It's a favourite, this one, rating tops for simplicity and flavour. Only a few special ingredients are required, but they are important to ensure that the dish ends up as it should – succulent, flavoursome, and so satisfying that you don't need pasta or potatoes or anything but a green salad to accompany it.

4 kabeljou (kob) fillets (about 180 g each, preferably the long, tail-end fillets)

fresh lemon juice

300 g bella (or baby plum) tomatoes, halved

6 spring onions, plus some tops, chopped

5 ml (1 tsp) Italian Herb Seasoning (mixed dried herbs)

200 g portabellini mushrooms, wiped and quartered

sea salt

60 ml (¼ cup) olive oil

60 ml (¼ cup) off-dry white wine

finely grated pecorino cheese and pine nuts for topping

Arrange the fillets, skin-side down, in a large baking dish or roaster, base-lined with baking paper. Be sure to leave plenty of room round the sides for the vegetables. Sprinkle the fish with a little lemon juice. Toss together the tomatoes, spring onions, dried herbs and mushrooms and when well mixed, scatter all round the fish – not on top. Sprinkle everything with salt, then mix the oil and wine and pour that over everything. Sprinkle the fish with a little of the cheese and then with pine nuts – just 5 ml (1 tsp) will do, per fillet. Now roast, uncovered, just below the centre of the oven at 200 C for about 25 minutes until the fish is cooked through and the tomatoes and mushrooms have started to shrivel and release their juices. Serve right away. **Serves 4.**

Poached Fish with Lemon & Tarragon

This is stove-top fish without any frying; the subtle, delicately flavoured sauce in no way spoils the purity of fresh, white fish fillets and it's easy enough to serve for a supper treat when everyone is tired of fish and chips. Furthermore, both the stock and the butter can be put together in advance, leaving only the fish requiring last-minute attention. You can serve it on mash – or leave off the starch and present simply with a mixed salad or stir-fried veg.

5 ml (1 tsp) very finely grated lemon rind (1 large lemon)

5 ml (1 tsp) dried tarragon

500 ml (2 cups) water

125 ml (½ cup) white wine

5 ml (1 tsp) sea salt

6 slices (about 1 kg) white fish fillets, skinned

20 ml (4 tsp) Dijon mustard

30 ml (2 Tbsp) flour

30 ml (2 Tbsp) soft butter

60 ml (¼ cup) reduced fat cream

Bring the lemon rind, tarragon, water, wine and salt to a slow boil in a very large, wide-based frying pan, then reduce the heat, cover and simmer for 10 minutes. Gently slide in the fish fillets, cover the pan, and poach gently until just cooked and the flesh flakes easily. Use a slotted spoon to transfer to a serving dish. Mash the mustard, flour and butter to a paste and add to the pan in single pats, while stirring. When thickened and smooth, swirl in the cream, then drizzle the sauce over the waiting fish. **Serves 6.**

Baked Fish Fillets on a Bed of Vegetables

This is a splendid way of transforming hake into something quite special without any fuss, frying or fancy ingredients. It's a good and useful recipe, which can be used with other kinds of fish as well, *except* for oily fish like snoek. Although hake seems to pop up mainly in fish pies or under a coat of batter, it's first choice here because its delicate flavour responds to this kind of treatment, and, being non-oily, it can take the topping of cheese and juicy sauce.

2 large onions, sliced across into thin rings

500 g ripe tomatoes, skinned and sliced into rings

sea salt, milled black pepper and a pinch of sugar

5 ml (1 tsp) dried dill, or dried tarragon, or mixed herbs

30 ml (2 Tbsp) olive oil

60 ml (¼ cup) white wine

4 fresh hake fillets (about 180 g each)

a little fresh lemon juice and sea salt

mozzarella cheese, grated

paprika

extra 60 ml (¼ cup) white wine

Brush a large baking dish with oil and arrange the onion slices in a single layer to cover the base. Top with the sliced tomatoes and sprinkle with the seasonings and dried herb of choice. Drizzle with the oil and wine, then bake uncovered at 180 ℃ for 15 minutes. Place the fish on top of the semi-soft vegetables, sprinkle lightly with lemon juice and salt, then top with cheese and a flurry of paprika. Pour the extra wine round – not on – the fish and bake, uncovered, at the same temperature, for about 20 minutes or until the fish is just cooked, the cheese melted, and the vegetables soft and juicy. To serve, spoon the veg over each fillet, or alongside, and serve with baby potatoes tossed in garlic butter, and a green vegetable – broccoli is good because of the bright colour. **Serves 4.**

Poached Fish with Anchovy Mayo & Crunchy Sage

This is a super alternative to that cold buffet special: a big, whole fish with head and tail on, the eye looking at you, and the body covered with sliced cucumber. In any case, not everyone has a big enough utensil for poaching a big, whole fish. For this recipe you need just a side of fish. Kabeljou (kob) is first choice. Slowly simmered in a delicate court bouillon, cooled, drizzled with the dressing and topped with fried sage leaves, it's deliciously different, and much easier than it sounds. You *do* need a very wide pan in which the fish can lie flat, and a side of kabeljou weighing 600–700 g, but otherwise it's plain sailing.

COURT BOUILLON

1.25 litres (5 cups) water

125 ml (½ cup) off-dry white wine

1 large carrot in 4 pieces

1 onion, chunkily chopped

2 bay leaves

a few black peppercorns

5 ml (1 tsp) sea salt

a few sprigs of parsley

ANCHOVY MAYONNAISE

1 x 40 g can flat fillets of anchovied sardines

125 ml (½ cup) thick mayonnaise

45 ml (3 Tbsp) thick Bulgarian yoghurt

a pinch of sugar

GARNISH

Heat a little oil in a frying pan and shallow-fry fresh sage leaves until they change colour and become crisp. Drain on paper towel and scatter over.

Bring all the bouillon ingredients to the boil, then cover and simmer for 30 minutes – you can do this in advance and leave to cool and draw flavour.

Place the fish, skin-side down, in your largest pan so that it lies flat. Strain the bouillon over the fish (it should be almost covered) and poach very, very gently until just cooked and opaque – white, no longer pink (add a dash of verjuice to the liquid if you have some handy). When done, remove from the heat and leave to cool in the bouillon. Use a spatula to transfer the fish, very carefully, to a large serving platter and drizzle with the anchovy mayo.

For the anchovy mayo, soak the anchovies for about 15 minutes in a little milk to tone down the salty flavour. Mix the remaining ingredients, then snip in the anchovies – you won't need the whole can, but most of it. Whisk to 'melt' a little – don't whizz in a blender – and leave the dressing slightly speckled. Drizzle over the fish, then sprinkle with 60 ml (4 Tbsp) chopped flat-leaf parsley mixed with 2 ml (½ tsp) finely grated lemon rind. Scatter the sage leaves over.

Unbelievably Easy Fish with Salsa

This is quite the most fuss-free and unpretentious dish – the sort of recipe one likes to turn to because it's so reliable and comfortable, like an old slipper. All you need is fresh hake and four ingredients to roll it in. Then, to jolly up the colour and flavour, quickly stir up a SALSA – avos and peppadews – and that's it.

30 ml (2 Tbsp) oil
20 ml (4 tsp) soy sauce
15 ml (1 Tbsp) white wine
5 ml (1 tsp) finely grated lemon rind
4 fresh, skinless hake fillets of equal thickness (about 550 g)
pre-roasted sesame seeds for topping

SALSA

peppadews (mild, whole, sweet piquanté peppers from a jar)
1 large avocado, peeled and diced
a dash of fresh lemon juice
3–4 spring onions, chopped
a pinch of sea salt and milled black pepper
5 ml (1 tsp) olive oil

Using a fork, mix the oil, soy sauce, wine and lemon rind on a large plate. Turn the fish fillets in the mixture several times to coat them well, then place in a baking dish lined with baking paper and pour over any remaining soy mixture. Sprinkle with sesame seeds and bake at 200 C for about 20 minutes, until just cooked through. If the juices have run, spoon them over the top of each fillet when serving, and pass a salt grinder – the soy sauce may season the fish sufficiently, but then again it may not, depending on the brand.

To make the salsa, snip enough peppadews (drained, rinsed) to give you 45–60 ml (3–4 Tbsp). Gently mix with the remaining ingredients, pile into a small bowl and serve with the fish. **Serves 4.**

Chicken, Brown Mushroom & Tomato Curry

The favourite.

15 ml (1 Tbsp) each oil and butter

8 large free-range chicken thighs (1 kg), trimmed

sea salt and milled black pepper

1 large onion, finely chopped

4 cloves garlic, crushed

30 ml (2 Tbsp) curry powder*

10 ml (2 tsp) ground cumin

5 ml (1 tsp) turmeric

15 ml (1 Tbsp) peeled, chopped fresh root ginger

250 g brown mushrooms, wiped and sliced

1 x 410 g can whole tomatoes, chopped, plus juice

2 fat sticks cinnamon

3 bay leaves

about 5 ml (1 tsp) sugar

45 ml (3 Tbsp) chutney

125 ml (½ cup) hot, seasoned chicken stock

a small handful of fresh coriander leaves

* Home-made curry powder can be spicy enough, so if this is what you're using, don't be too generous with the above additions.

Heat the oil and butter in a large frying pan and brown the chicken on both sides – fry skin side first to release the fat. Transfer to a large baking dish and remove the crisped skins – this allows the chicken to absorb the flavours better and avoids a greasy sauce. Turn skinned sides down and season lightly. The thighs should fit fairly closely, but allow space for the chunky sauce – a deep, 28 x 22 cm dish is just right. Add the onion, garlic, all the ground spices and the ginger to the pan drippings and sauté briefly over low heat – if the drippings are quickly absorbed, add a dash of water. Add the mushrooms, toss until mixed with the spices, then add the remaining ingredients, except the coriander. Bring to the boil, stirring, then pour over the chicken – the pieces should be almost completely covered. Tuck the cinnamon and bay leaves right in, cover securely (grease-proof paper and then a sheet of foil) and bake at 160 C for 1 hour 15 minutes. Turn the chicken and bake, uncovered, for a further 15 minutes or until tender and the sauce is nicely reduced. Use a slotted spoon to transfer the thighs to a heated serving dish, remove the bay leaves and cinnamon sticks from the sauce, swirl in the coriander, pour over the chicken and serve with a fragrant rice and thick yoghurt – plain, or spiked with grated radishes and a chilli or two. **Serves 4–6.**

Chicken Thighs Baked on a Bed of Vegetables

There's a lovely harmony of tastes and textures in this bright chicken dish, which is initially baked covered, to seal in all the flavours and juices, and then uncovered in order to brown the chicken. The completed dish is a picture to make your mouth water – and although the assembly time is quite lengthy, once it's done you can relax.

2 medium onions, peeled and quartered

300 g baby marrows, pared and sliced into strips

1 large red pepper, seeded, ribs removed, and sliced

2 x 200 g brinjals, scrubbed and cubed*

400 g tomatoes (skin on), quartered

200 g brown mushrooms, wiped and thickly sliced

12 cloves garlic, unpeeled

60 ml (¼ cup) olive oil

sea salt, milled black pepper and a large pinch of sugar

3–4 sprigs fresh rosemary

6 large free-range chicken thighs (800 g), trimmed of excess fat

paprika and dried oregano

Use a very large, deep baking dish, round about 36 x 26 x 5 cm. Add all the vegetables, toss with 45 ml (3 Tbsp) of the oil (use your hands), and when glistening, season and tuck in the rosemary. Place the chicken thighs, skin side up, on the vegetables, not too close to each other, and push them down very gently – they must *not* be smothered. Salt them lightly and sprinkle with paprika and oregano. Cover securely, first with a sheet of greaseproof paper and then foil, and bake at 160 C for 1 hour. Uncover and bake for 45 minutes, or until the chicken is gloriously brown and tender, in a succulent sauce. Remove the rosemary, and serve the chicken and veg on rice or couscous to soak up the juices. Don't forget to locate the garlic cloves: place two on each plate so that diners can squeeze the mellow flesh into the vegetables. **Serves 6.**

* If using one large brinjal it should be dégorged: scrub, cube, sprinkle with salt, place in a colander with a weight on top, leave for about 40 minutes while the bitter juices run out, then rinse well and dry thoroughly (a salad spinner does the job perfectly).

Chicken & Mango Salad

An eye-catching combination of bright ingredients goes into this salad of chicken poached in apple juice, mixed into a creamy curry sauce together with fresh mangoes, and finished off with nuts and coriander. It's as good as it sounds, is not difficult to prepare, and can be made in advance and refrigerated overnight. Serve with a rice or couscous salad and a mild fruit chutney – atchars would be too strong for the delicate flavour of this salad.

500–600 g free-range skinless chicken breast fillets

250 ml (1 cup) apple juice

2 whole cloves

a little sea salt

1 stick cinnamon

2 medium, firm but ripe fibreless mangoes, peeled and diced

chopped walnuts or pecans and fresh coriander to garnish

DRESSING

30 ml (2 Tbsp) oil

1 medium onion, finely chopped

15 ml (1 Tbsp) curry powder

5 ml (1 tsp) turmeric

125 ml (½ cup) reserved chicken stock

125 ml (½ cup) mayonnaise

125 ml (½ cup) sour cream OR thick Bulgarian yoghurt

Poach the chicken gently in apple juice with the cloves, salt and cinnamon for about 10 minutes, or until just cooked. Cool in the stock, then slice the chicken into thin strips across the grain. Strain the stock and reserve. To make the dressing, heat the oil in a small saucepan. Add the onion and let it soften without browning. Add the spices and sizzle for a minute, then add the reserved stock and simmer uncovered until the mixture thickens – this happens quite quickly. Press through a sieve, discard the onion, and stir the smooth sauce into the mayonnaise mixed with the sour cream or yoghurt. Fold in the chicken, then the mango, spoon into a glass container, cover and refrigerate. Before serving, check the seasoning and, if too sweet, sharpen with a little fresh lemon juice. Spoon onto a beautiful platter, and garnish with the nuts and a generous sprinkling of coriander leaves. **Serves 6–8.**

Finger-licking Chicken Wings

Chicken wings are often neglected – I suppose because there's not much meat on them – but they're succulent and jolly useful. In the following recipe they're marinated in a barbecue-type sauce, which adds great colour and flavour. Once cooked, they can be served as an economical main course with the juices spooned over, accompanied by baked potatoes and sour cream; alternatively, drain off the juices and serve with drinks; or grill over the coals and pass them round for nibbling, to appease appetites.

1 kg free-range chicken wings
30 ml (2 Tbsp) oil
45 ml (3 Tbsp) sweet sherry
45 ml (3 Tbsp) tomato sauce
30 ml (2 Tbsp) fresh lemon juice
5 ml (1 tsp) Worcestershire sauce
15 ml (1 Tbsp) soy sauce
10 ml (2 tsp) pale, runny honey
10 ml (2 tsp) curry powder
10 ml (2 tsp) chilli sauce (or more for extra bite)
sea salt and milled black pepper

Remove the wing tips if your butcher has not already done so, then pull the wings apart and cut through at the joint, making two pieces. Be careful not to cut through the bone, leaving a jagged edge, but at the precise point where the joint separates. Arrange in a single layer in a large glass or porcelain baking dish – 30 x 24 cm is ideal. Mix the remaining ingredients, except the salt and pepper, pour over the wings and leave to stand for 30 minutes at room temperature, or refrigerate for up to 6 hours, turning several times. Unless using a fridge-to-oven baking dish, return to room temperature before baking. Season very lightly, and bake, uncovered, at 180 C for 25 minutes. Turn the pieces over and add a little water to the baking dish if necessary, to prevent scorching. Reduce the heat to 160 C and bake for a further 25 minutes, or until tender, browned and juicy.
Makes about 32 pieces, serving 5–6 as a main.

Chicken Casserole with Mushrooms & Red Wine

An unpretentious but deliciously satisfying chicken dish, with a full-bodied flavour.
The ingredients are quite basic, and the preparation not too quick, but straightforward.

12 pickling onions, peeled

1 kg free-range chicken thighs,
trimmed of excess fat

2 ml (½ tsp) each salt and paprika

1 small onion, chopped

1 red pepper, seeded, ribs removed,
and diced

250 g brown mushrooms, wiped
and sliced

2 ml (½ tsp) dried thyme

30 ml (2 Tbsp) flour

250 ml (1 cup) chicken stock

100 ml (⅖ cup) robust red wine

15 ml (1 Tbsp) tomato paste

2 ml (½ tsp) sea salt and a little sugar

5 ml (1 tsp) Worcestershire sauce

Cut a cross through the root end of each pickling onion, arrange in a single layer in a large frying pan, half-cover with cold, lightly salted water, add a pinch of sugar and bring to the boil. Reduce the heat and simmer for about 8 minutes, then drain and set aside. (Don't boil rapidly, or overcook, as they must retain their shape.) Smear the base of a frying pan with a little oil and lightly brown the chicken on both sides – do the skin side first, to release the fat. Arrange the thighs, skin side up, in a baking dish to fit, and sprinkle with salt and paprika. Cover with a lid, or a sheet of greaseproof paper and then one of foil, and bake at 160 C for 30 minutes. Meanwhile, make the sauce. Add the chopped onion and red pepper to the pan drippings and sauté briefly. Add the mushrooms and thyme and a little extra oil if necessary, and stir-fry until softened. Sprinkle in the flour, tossing to mix, then add the remaining ingredients, stirring until the sauce thickens. Remove the chicken from the oven, uncover, and pour off the fat. Pour the sauce over, and tuck in the parboiled pickling onions. Cover as before and bake for a further 45 minutes or until the chicken is tender. **Serves 4–6.**

Favourite Quick Chicken

This lemony, herby, spicy chicken (memories of the Med) is just the best when it comes to kitchen blues. When dinner is required and you are absolutely *not* in the mood for pots and wooden spoons, your energy is flagging and you'd rather be in the garden, let this recipe save you.

800 g free-range chicken thighs, trimmed of excess fat

a little sea salt

MARINADE

60 ml (¼ cup) fresh lemon juice

30 ml (2 Tbsp) olive oil

30 ml (2 Tbsp) brandy

15 ml (1 Tbsp) runny honey

2 cloves garlic, crushed

7 ml (1½ tsp) ground cumin

7 ml (1½ tsp) dried oregano

2 ml (½ tsp) ground cinnamon

Arrange the chicken in a baking dish to fit closely. Mix all the ingredients for the marinade, pour over the chicken and refrigerate for 1–4 hours, turning a few times. Unless using a fridge-to-oven baking dish, return to room temperature before baking. Arrange the thighs skin side up, salt lightly, and bake, uncovered, at 160 C for 45 minutes. Baste with the juices in the dish, then continue baking for a further 25 minutes or until the chicken is browned and tender. Transfer to a warmed platter and pour the juices over. **Serves 4.**

Spicy Chicken Curry

A perennial favourite, abundantly perfumed and flavoured.

45 ml (3 Tbsp) flour

7 ml (1½ tsp) salt

5 ml (1 tsp) garam masala

8 large, free-range, skinless chicken thighs (not less than 1 kg)*

30 ml (2 Tbsp) oil

2 medium onions, chopped

2–3 cloves garlic, crushed

10 ml (2 tsp) chopped, peeled fresh root ginger

15 ml (1 Tbsp) curry powder

5 ml (1 tsp) each ground cumin and turmeric

3 whole star anise

2 sticks cinnamon

300 ml (1⅕ cups) chicken stock

125 ml (½ cup) tomato puré

2 bay leaves

60 ml (4 Tbsp) seedless raisins

30 ml (2 Tbsp) chutney

fresh coriander leaves to garnish

Mix the flour, salt and masala, rub it into the chicken, arrange in a lightly oiled baking dish to fit quite snugly and sprinkle over any remaining flour mixture. Heat the oil, add the onions and garlic and fry lightly, then add all the spices and stir over low heat until the aroma escapes – if necessary, add a dash of water to prevent scorching. Add the remaining ingredients, except the garnish, stir while heating through, then pour the sauce over the chicken. Check that the spices lie in the sauce and not on top of the thighs, then cover securely with a lid or a sheet of greaseproof paper and then one of foil, and bake at 160 C for 45 minutes. Turn the chicken, cover again, and bake for a further 30 minutes, or until tender. Remove the whole spices and bay leaves, transfer to a heated serving dish and sprinkle with coriander leaves. **Serves 4–6.**

* **Skinless thighs absorb flavours readily and ensure a non-fatty sauce.**

Orange Coq Au Vin

A simplified version of the classic dish, with a new flip to the flavour.

15 ml (1 Tbsp) oil and a dab of butter
1 kg free-range chicken portions,
preferably trimmed thighs
and drumsticks
sea salt and milled black pepper
3–4 rashers lean shoulder
bacon, diced
12 pickling onions, peeled
2–3 cloves garlic, crushed
30 ml (2 Tbsp) flour
2 ml (½ tsp) dried thyme
175 ml (⅔ cup) red wine
125 ml (½ cup) fresh orange juice
5 ml (1 tsp) finely grated orange rind
30 ml (2 Tbsp) brandy
15 ml (1 Tbsp) tomato paste
60 ml (¼ cup) chicken stock
5 ml (1 tsp) honey
2 bay leaves
200 g button mushrooms, halved
chopped parsley to garnish

Heat the oil and butter and brown the chicken on both sides. Remove to a baking dish – not too large, or the sauce will boil away, but large enough to take the rather bulky ingredients. Season. Over low heat, toss the bacon, onions and garlic in the pan drippings and, when the onions are lightly browned, sprinkle in the flour and the thyme, crushed between the fingers. When absorbed, add the remaining ingredients, except the mushrooms and garnish. Stir until boiling, then pour the sauce over the chicken, tucking in the onions. Cover securely with a lid or with a sheet of greaseproof paper and then one of foil, and bake at 160 C for 1 hour 15 minutes. Stir in the mushrooms and bake, uncovered, for 15 minutes. Use a paper towel to blot up any little greasy blobs, remove the bay leaves and sprinkle with parsley. **Serves 4–5.**

Quick Mushroom Chicken

An old-timer, slipped in again because it's so eternally useful: breast fillets quickly simmered in a delicately flavoured sauce with a hint of tarragon and sherry, and a little cream to round it off. The whole operation takes about twenty minutes and this makes the dish a real pleasure to prepare at the end of a busy day. Instead of reducing the sauce by rapid boiling, it is thickened with cornflour – not a gourmet practice, but convenient, and the breasts turn out plump and succulent. So it's easy, and good.

30 ml (2 Tbsp) oil

5 ml (1 tsp) butter

6 skinless chicken breast fillets (about 600 g)

6 slim spring onions, chopped

7 ml (1½ tsp) dried tarragon

60 ml (¼ cup) sweet sherry (OB's is perfect)

250 ml (1 cup) hot chicken stock

10 ml (2 tsp) tomato paste

250 g button mushrooms, wiped and sliced

a little sea salt

10 ml (2 tsp) cornflour

60 ml (¼ cup) fresh cream (reduced fat cream works very well)

You'll need a really large frying pan so that nothing need be done in relays. Heat the oil and butter, make three diagonal slashes on the skinned sides of the breasts, and quickly seal on both sides; don't brown them – they should just turn white on the outsides and remain very pink underneath. Remove from the pan, reduce the heat, add the spring onions, tarragon and sherry, stir until almost evaporated, then add the stock, tomato paste, mushrooms and salt. Stir until just bubbling, then return the chicken, cover, and simmer over very low heat for about 10 minutes or until just cooked through, turning once. Slake the cornflour with the cream, add to the pan and simmer for a minute or two to make a medium-thick sauce, stirring gently to combine. Check the seasoning. **Serves 6.**

Chicken Breasts Stuffed with Spinach & Ricotta

There are four steps to this recipe: mixing the stuffing, slipping it into the breasts, making the tomato sauce, then adding the chicken and simmering until cooked. This does take a little time, but the result is a different way with chicken breasts using Italian-style ingredients. Plenty of flavour and colour, and good with buttered noodles and a green salad.

100 g baby spinach leaves

100 g ricotta cheese

2 ml (½ tsp) freshly grated nutmeg

a large pinch of sea salt

6 skinless chicken breast fillets
(about 600 g)

shavings of parmesan or pecorino
cheese for topping

SAUCE

1 x 410 g can Italian-style
sliced tomatoes

4–6 spring onions, chopped

1 large carrot, very finely diced

300 ml (1⅕ cups) chicken stock

30 ml (2 Tbsp) olive oil

2–3 cloves garlic, crushed

5 ml (1 tsp) tomato paste

a handful of chopped parsley

5–10 ml (1–2 tsp) sugar

Pour boiling water over the spinach, leave to stand for 5 minutes, then drain very well in a colander; press down hard with a wooden spoon until absolutely dry – pat with a paper towel to make sure – then chop – you should have 60 ml (¼ cup) packed solid. Using a fork, mash the spinach with the ricotta and seasonings. Using a sharp knife, cut a deep vertical slit in the plump side of each chicken breast, being careful not to puncture the flaps. Ease open, and smooth a heaped tablespoon of the stuffing into each pocket, then close the flap and pinch securely – no need to skewer. If working ahead, refrigerate. Make the tomato sauce by mixing all the ingredients in a very large pan, wide enough to take the breasts later on, without crowding. Bring to the boil, then reduce the heat and simmer, covered, for about 30 minutes, stirring occasionally, until fairly thick and the flavours have mellowed – salt is not usually necessary. Carefully add the chicken, ladle some sauce over each breast, then cover and simmer for 10 minutes. Turn carefully, then continue to simmer until cooked through – about 20 minutes altogether. Serve the chicken on heated plates with the sauce spooned over, and topped with a sprinkling of cheese to round it all off. **Serves 6.**

Chocolate-Chilli Chicken

The chilli bites only slightly, the chocolate is only subtly there, but the combination of ingredients adds up to an unusual medley of flavours that come as a happy surprise, because the dish *looks* like chicken in a richly-coloured sauce … yet it definitely is more than that. Serve with couscous and a green salad with avo, and use skinless chicken thigh fillets. They *are* available, and the dish is simply not the same using other cuts.

375 ml (1½ cups) chicken stock

2 red chillies, seeded and chopped

200 g tomatoes, skinned, seeds flicked out, and chopped

½ bunch spring onions, or 3 baby leeks, chopped

2 ml (½ tsp) ground coriander

1 ml (¼ tsp) ground cinnamon

a little sea salt and a good pinch of sugar

30 ml (2 Tbsp) lightly pre-toasted, crushed almond flakes (use a rolling pin)

45 ml (3 Tbsp) finely grated dark chocolate (about 15 g)

14 skinless chicken thigh fillets (about 650 g)

fresh coriander leaves to garnish

Place the stock, chillies, tomatoes, spring onions or leeks, spices and seasonings in a blender goblet and whizz until well mixed – it won't be absolutely smooth. Pour into a large jug and stir in the almonds and chocolate. Smear a very large, wide frying pan with oil and seal the chicken quickly on both sides (keep them doubled over to save space). Pour the sauce over, bring to the boil (smell the chocolate), then reduce the heat, cover and simmer gently until tender and cooked through – about 30 minutes – these little nuggets do not take long. The next step is a bit of a nuisance, but necessary. Using a slotted spoon, remove the chicken, turn the heat up and reduce the sauce by rapid boiling – it becomes bubbly and suitably thickened very quickly. Return the chicken and sprinkle with lots of coriander.

Serves 5–6.

Butter Bean, Mushroom & Walnut Curry

This easy, stove-top dish with its rather unusual ingredients is just fabulous. It has quite a lively tang, and a rather surprising colour – pale caramel – which looks surprisingly good on fragrant yellow rice. It's easy to double up on the ingredients, which might be a wise step, as second helpings are usually called for.

45 ml (3 Tbsp) oil
1 large onion, finely chopped
½–1 small fresh red chilli, seeded and shredded
15 ml (1 Tbsp) curry powder
2 ml (½ tsp) each ground cumin, cinnamon and turmeric
45 ml (3 Tbsp) flour
250 ml (1 cup) hot vegetable stock
250 ml (1 cup) milk (preferably low-fat)
a little sea salt and a pinch of sugar
15 ml (1 Tbsp) tomato paste
200 g brown mushrooms, wiped and coarsely chopped
1 red pepper, seeded, ribs removed, and diced
125 ml (½ cup) coarsely chopped walnuts
1 x 400 g can choice-grade butter beans, drained and rinsed
fresh lemon juice

First make the sauce by heating the oil in a wide-based, heavy saucepan or large frying pan. Add the onion and chilli and fry very lightly, then add the spices and sizzle for a minute. Sprinkle in the flour, stirring to mix and adding a dash of water if dry, then slowly stir in the stock and milk. Allow to thicken over low heat, then add the seasoning and tomato paste. Cover and simmer, keeping the heat low – the sauce should just pop – for about 10 minutes, stirring occasionally to prevent sticking. Meanwhile, sauté the mushrooms, red pepper and walnuts in 15 ml (1 Tbsp) each oil and butter until the mushrooms are just softening but still chunky, then stir them into the sauce along with the beans, and simmer until heated through, OR omit this step and simply add these ingredients to the sauce and simmer until the mushrooms are cooked. Check the seasoning, and add a little extra stock if necessary – the mixture should be really moist – and add a dash of lemon juice to sharpen the flavour. Serve with chutney and a green salad. **Serves 4–5.**

Baked Rice & Vegetables with Omelette Topping

In this meatless dish (absolutely bursting with good things), the vegetables are first sautéd and then baked with the uncooked rice and herbs, resulting in maximum flavour with the minimum of fuss and a lovely aroma while it is in the oven. The omelette, sliced into strips for the topping, finishes it off beautifully. Serve with a tossed green salad.

60 ml (¼ cup) oil
1 onion, chopped
2 leeks (white part only), sliced
2 cloves garlic, crushed
250 g brown mushrooms, wiped and sliced
4 young carrots, julienned
2 sticks celery, plus some leaves, chopped
375 ml (1½ cups) uncooked brown rice, rinsed
125 ml (½ cup) chopped parsley
800 ml (3⅕ cups) hot vegetable or Marmite stock
sea salt and milled black pepper
30–45 ml (2–3 Tbsp) finely chopped fresh herbs*
30 ml (2 Tbsp) soy sauce
125 ml (½ cup) toasted slivered almonds
a few pats of butter

Heat the oil in a large pan and lightly fry the onion, leeks and garlic. Add the mushrooms, carrots and celery and stir-fry for a few minutes until glistening, smelling good and starting to soften. Spoon into a 20 x 30 cm baking dish, add the rice, parsley, stock, seasoning and herbs, stir to mix well, then cover and bake at 160 C for about 1 hour 10 minutes, or until the rice is cooked and the stock absorbed. Fork in the soy sauce, almonds and butter.

OMELETTES

Make these a few minutes before the dish is done. Lightly mix 8–10 free-range eggs with a little water, salt and pepper. Cook half the mixture in an omelette pan (or lightly oiled frying pan) at a time. When just set, tilt the pan and roll the omelette over a few times, slide onto a plate and slice thinly; cook the second omelette, and arrange the slices on top of the rice dish as it comes out of the oven. **Serves 6.**

* **A good mixture: rosemary, thyme, marjoram and oregano.**

Chickpea Curry with Mango & Mint Raita

A mild, spicy, super vegetarian dish; serve on fragrant rice.

30 ml (2 Tbsp) oil

1 large onion, finely chopped

2–3 cloves garlic, crushed

1 yellow pepper, seeded, ribs removed, and sliced

20 ml (4 tsp) curry powder (or more)

5 ml (1 tsp) each ground cumin and coriander

2 ml (½ tsp) each ground cinnamon and turmeric

500 g really ripe tomatoes, skinned and chopped*

375 ml (1½ cups) vegetable stock

15 ml (1 Tbsp) tomato paste

2 bay leaves

a little sea salt

a trickle of runny honey

750 ml (3 cups) cooked chickpeas OR 2 x 400 g cans, drained and rinsed

a handful of chopped parsley

roasted cashew nuts, chopped, for topping (optional)

Heat the oil in a large saucepan, add the onion, garlic and yellow pepper and, when softening, add all the spices. Stir briefly to release the flavours, adding, if necessary, a dash of water to prevent scorching. Stir in the remaining ingredients, except the cashews, bring to the boil, then cover and simmer very gently for about 35 minutes. Stir occasionally to mash up the tomatoes. Check seasoning, and if the sauce needs thickening, tilt the lid of the saucepan for the last few minutes. Remove the bay leaves, spoon into a heated serving dish and top with the cashews, if using. **Serves 4–6.**

* A 400 g can (plus the juice) could, at a pinch be substituted, but in this case you will probably have to reduce the amount of stock by about 125 ml (½ cup).

Mango & Mint Raita

For the raita, mix 250 ml (1 cup) thick Bulgarian yoghurt (low fat or fat free), a few chopped spring onions, a pinch of salt, about 125 ml (½ cup) diced, ripe mango and shredded fresh mint leaves (start with 12) in a small bowl, cover and refrigerate while the curry cooks. Just before serving, sprinkle with garam masala.

Green Risotto with Butternut, Pine Nuts & Asparagus

An unusual risotto, a novel colour, and a memorable taste experience.

400 g butternut, peeled, cut into small dice (prepared weight)
a good sprinkling of ground cinnamon
a trickle of runny honey
1.125 litres (4½ cups) vegetable stock
enough Swiss chard, cooked and well drained, to provide 125 ml (½ cup) tightly packed
1 large onion, finely chopped
45 ml (3 Tbsp) each olive oil and butter
375 ml (1½ cups) arborio rice
2 ml (½ tsp) freshly grated nutmeg
45 ml (3 Tbsp) freshly grated parmesan or pecorino cheese
sea salt to taste
poached asparagus and toasted pine nuts for topping

Cook the butternut in the minimum of salted water – use a wide frying pan, spread it out in a single layer, sprinkle with cinnamon, drizzle with honey, and simmer until just tender. Set aside. Blend the stock and cooked Swiss chard in a blender (probably in two batches) until smooth and about as green as lucerne. Heat it. Soften the onion in the oil and butter in a large, deep saucepan, add the rice and nutmeg, toss to coat, then add the hot stock slowly, in small doses, waiting until each dose is absorbed before stirring in another. Don't hurry the process – be prepared to stand there for about 30 minutes, by which time the rice should be creamy. Carefully fold in the butternut plus any juices left in its pan, then, off the heat, fold in the cheese and salt to taste. Cover with a cloth and leave for a few minutes before ladling into deep bowls or soup plates. Pass the asparagus and pine nuts in separate bowls. Extra parmesan makes a good but optional addition. **Serves 6, with a salad.**

Quick Chilli Beans with Corn & Avocado

This is one of those speedy suppers that doesn't fall down on flavour despite the haste. You simply mix the ingredients for the sauce in a saucepan, and while they're in there simmering you open the beans and slice the avocado. Best served on couscous, but brown rice is also good.

½–2 red chillies, chopped*
1 small green pepper, seeded, ribs removed, and diced
1 x 400 g can chopped tomatoes in juice**
1–2 cloves garlic, crushed
30 ml (2 Tbsp) soft brown sugar
1 small onion, finely chopped
125 ml (½ cup) water
15 ml (1 Tbsp) red wine vinegar
a large pinch of sea salt
1 x 400 g can choice-grade butter beans, drained and rinsed
250 ml (1 cup) cooked corn kernels (use fresh or frozen)
1 avocado, thinly segmented
milled black pepper to taste

To make the sauce you'll need a large, deep frying pan as the beans get added to it and butter beans are voluptuously plump. Combine the chillies, green pepper, tomatoes, garlic, sugar, onion, water, vinegar and salt in the pan. Stir to mix, bring to the boil, immediately reduce the heat, cover and simmer very gently for about 30 minutes until slightly thickened. Add the beans and the corn and simmer for 5–10 minutes, until very hot. Check seasoning, turn into a heated serving dish, top prettily with the avo (which is not a garnish, it is important to the dish), grind over the pepper and serve. I also like a splosh of yoghurt on the side – it cools the chilli and the colour contrast is pleasing. **Serves 4, easily doubled.**

* Chillies differ enormously with regard to heat – it depends on the colour, the size, and whether you add the seeds or not. The amount and type of chilli used here depends on the choice of the cook, so it's a good idea to swot them up.
** These differ slightly in density from cans of whole peeled tomatoes – they are interchangeable, but you might have to adjust the quantity of liquid in the recipe.

Simply Splendid Vegetable Curry

This one would feel right at home in the Karoo – simple country cooking, using pumpkin and sweet potatoes and spices and chutney – all adding up to a fragrant supper dish on one of those winter evenings when, if you set foot outside, the air will bite your nose and freeze your fingers off.

45 ml (3 Tbsp) oil and a pat of butter
1 large onion, chopped
3 cloves garlic, chopped
15 ml (1 Tbsp) finely chopped, peeled root ginger
30 ml (2 Tbsp) curry powder
5 ml (1 tsp) each ground cumin and turmeric
300 g peeled, cubed pumpkin or butternut (peeled weight)*
300 g peeled, cubed sweet potatoes (peeled weight)
1 x 410 g can whole tomatoes, chopped, plus juice
45 ml (3 Tbsp) chutney
250 ml (1 cup) vegetable stock
1 fat stick cinnamon
a handful of chopped parsley
sea salt to taste
250–300 g small broccoli florets
fresh lemon juice
roasted cashew nuts and garam masala for topping

Heat the oil and butter in a very large, deep frying pan (about 28 x 7 cm) and sauté the onion, garlic and ginger. Add the spices and cook for a minute, then add the pumpkin (or butternut) and sweet potatoes, and toss to mix with the spices – add a dash of water if the mixture seems dry. Add the remaining ingredients except the broccoli, lemon juice, cashews and garam masala. Stir to mix, then cover and simmer over very low heat for about 30 minutes until the vegetables are nearly cooked. Gently stir in the broccoli and simmer, covered, until the vegetables are tender, but holding their shape and the juices reduced and slightly thickened. Much depends on the size of your pan – you might have to add extra stock – up to 250 ml (1 cup). Add a dash of lemon juice to bring out the flavour, remove the cinnamon, spoon the curry into a large, heated serving dish and top with the nuts and a sprinkling of garam masala.
Serves 6.

* Be sure to use a pumpkin that has firm, bright orange flesh – if yours is pale and watery, put it away – and reach for a butternut instead.

Roasted Vegetable & Pasta Party Salad

A magnificent party salad: a medley of vegetables, marinated in oil with fresh herbs, roasted until succulent, then tossed with pasta. It can be made a day ahead and refrigerated. Serve mounded on a platter, dotted with black olives and crumbled feta, with a warm flat bread on the side.

500 g brinjals, cubed and degorged

3 large yellow peppers (300 g), seeded, ribs removed, and sliced

500 g baby marrows, pared and julienned

250–300 g brown mushrooms, wiped and chunkily chopped

2–4 slender leeks, wiped and sliced into 4 cm pieces

100 ml (⅖ cup) each olive and canola or sunflower oil

3 cloves garlic, crushed

45 ml (3 Tbsp) fresh lemon juice

5 ml (1 tsp) each sea salt and sugar

4 large sprigs *each* fresh rosemary, thyme and marjoram

250 g broccoli florets

375 ml (1½ cups) elbow macaroni

Place the brinjals, yellow peppers, baby marrows, mushrooms and leeks in a very large porcelain baking dish, about 27 x 22 x 7 cm. Mix the oils, garlic, lemon juice, salt and sugar and pour over. Tuck in the herbs and toss to mix everything together, then cover and leave to stand for about 2 hours, tossing when you think of it. Roast, uncovered, at 220 C for 20 minutes. Remove from the oven, toss to mix, then reduce the temperature to 180 C and bake for a further 20 minutes or until the vegetables are juicy and tender. Discard the stalks of herbs – most of the leaves will have fallen off, adding their flavour to the juices. Steam the broccoli until just tender, and drain. Cook the pasta, then drain. Mix these with the vegetables and set aside to cool. Garnish as suggested above and serve at room temperature, or refrigerate (in glass) overnight, then garnish just before serving. **Serves 8–10.**

Pasta Puttanesca Salad with Basil Oil

This zesty pasta dish is usually served hot, but it also makes a vibrant salad – great at a summer buffet or patio supper. Puttanesca sauce is a rather strange mixture – plenty of the ubiquitous tomatoes, but with anchovies, chillies and olives making it rather different from most pasta sauces, while the dark, dense basil oil is a personal twist that adds both richness and flavour.

30 ml (2 Tbsp) olive oil

1 x 50 g can flat fillets of anchovied sardines, drained and briefly soaked in milk*

1 bunch of spring onions or 6 baby leeks, sliced

2 cloves garlic, crushed

2 x 400 g cans chopped tomatoes in juice

12 black olives, pitted and slivered

1–2 fresh chillies, seeded and chopped

1 large yellow pepper, seeded, ribs removed, and thinly sliced

a handful of flat-leaf parsley

a little sea salt and about 10 ml (2 tsp) sugar **

250 g fusilli tricolore

BASIL OIL

30 g fresh basil leaves, washed, dried

250 ml (1 cup) oil – half olive and half canola or sunflower

a small pinch each of sugar and salt

* Used for convenience as these cans are readily available.

Using a wide-based frying pan, heat the olive oil with the oil from the drained anchovies. Add the spring onions or leeks and garlic and stir for a minute, then add the remaining ingredients, except the pasta. Simmer over low heat, uncovered, stirring often until it has thickened. Taste. If not hot enough, add a sprinkling of crushed dried chillies. Simmer 10 minutes more. Meanwhile, cook the pasta, drain and turn into a large serving dish. Add the sauce, toss to combine well, then stand uncovered to cool – the sauce will gradually be absorbed. Cover and leave for up to 2 hours, or turn into a glass bowl and refrigerate overnight.

Blend all the basil oil ingredients well – the result will be a dark, strongly flavoured oil, which really adds something special to the salad. Pass round in a jug, to be trickled (sparingly) over each serving. (Can also be refrigerated overnight.) You could also pass a bowl of grated pecorino, which would make the meal really rich and robust. **Serves 6.**

** This might seem like a lot of sugar, but canned tomatoes are tart and really need long, low simmering to mellow them. As the cooking time in this recipe is relatively short, you will need a little extra sweetness.

Pasta, Bean & Rocket Salad with Pine Nuts

A bright, succulent mixture of colourful fusilli tossed up with stir-fried vegetables; added substance comes from the borlotti beans, and lots of flavour from the rocket, cheese and nuts. Super for lunch, with a leafy salad and a hunk of flat bread.

75 ml (5 Tbsp) olive oil
4–6 spring onions, chopped
2 cloves garlic, crushed
1 red pepper, seeded, ribs removed, and julienned
125 g baby marrows, pared and julienned
125–250 g button mushrooms, wiped and chunkily chopped
sea salt and milled black pepper
15 ml (1 Tbsp) balsamic vinegar
200 g fusilli tricolore (mixed pasta screws)
1 x 400 g can borlotti beans, drained and rinsed
30 g (about 500 ml/2 cups) rocket, torn
75 ml (5 Tbsp) grated parmesan or pecorino cheese
45–60 ml (3–4 Tbsp) roasted pine nuts*

Heat the oil in a large frying pan, add the spring onions, garlic, red pepper and baby marrows and stir-fry for a few minutes before adding the mushrooms. Toss until softening, then remove from the stove, season, and add the vinegar. Tip the just-cooked and drained (not rinsed) pasta into a large bowl, add the beans, the stir-fry mixture with all its juices, and the rocket. Toss gently until combined, cool, then cover loosely and leave for an hour or so.** Just before serving, fork in the cheese and check the seasoning. Serve on a big platter, topped with the nuts. **Serves 6.**

* The pine nuts are not listed as a garnish as they are an integral part of the salad, but because they're so expensive you want to see them, and that is why they're on top. When roasting, do it properly – that is, let them get really nut-brown – it makes a huge difference to the flavour.

** This salad should be served at room temperature. If you have to make it in advance, it can be refrigerated (covered) for up to a day, but it will lose out on the fine flavour.

Pasta Stroganoff

Also known as Slimmer's Stroganoff because the sour cream used in traditional stroganoff has been left out, but it's actually nowhere near a slimming dish – what mix of fried steak in a thick, creamy gravy can possibly be? Nevertheless, it has its virtues: it stretches a little fillet to feed a lot, it's a change from bolognaise, and the flavour is good. Serve on tagliatelle or fettucine, with a big green salad for a no-frills party dish.

600 g fillet of beef

20 ml (4 tsp) Worcestershire sauce

3–4 cloves garlic, crushed

2 ml (½ tsp) dried thyme, crushed

30 ml (2 Tbsp) oil

250 g brown mushrooms, wiped and sliced

1 large bunch of spring onions, chopped

500 ml (2 cups) low-fat milk

30 ml (2 Tbsp) tomato paste

25 ml (5 tsp) soy sauce

a pinch each of sea salt and sugar

20 ml (4 tsp) cornflour

45 ml (3 Tbsp) medium-dry sherry

Slice the beef across the grain into wafer-thin strips – most easily done if the beef is semi-frozen. Place in a large, shallow dish, add the Worcestershire sauce, garlic and thyme, toss to mix, then cover loosely and leave to stand for 45 minutes. Heat the oil in a large frying pan and stir-fry the steak briefly, until just browned, tossing all the time. Add the mushrooms and spring onions, and keep tossing over medium heat until softening, then turn the heat to very low and add the milk, tomato paste, soy sauce, salt and sugar. Stir to mix, then cover and simmer very gently for 4–5 minutes. Mix the cornflour with the sherry, stir into the pan and allow to boil up, stirring, until the sauce has smoothed out and thickened. **Serves 6.**

Pasta with Smoked Salmon, Mushrooms & Cream

I'm not a fan of smoked foods, but salmon is my downfall. Eat it with pasta in a restaurant, however, and it is often so richly extravagant one would not consider making it at home – not often, anyway. Now this recipe was devised with an eye to scaling the whole lot down – mushrooms to pad it out and milk and cornflour (I blush, I blush) to dilute the cream – and it really works rather well despite the liberties taken.

500 g button mushrooms, wiped and thinly sliced
6–8 spring onions, chopped
250 ml (1 cup) fresh cream
250 ml (1 cup) milk
125 ml (½ cup) off-dry white wine
30 ml (2 Tbsp) tomato paste
a little sea salt
30 ml (2 Tbsp) cornflour
about 320 g smoked salmon, sliced into thin strips
400 g pasta screws

Put the mushrooms and spring onions into a large saucepan. In a separate bowl, stir together the cream, milk, wine, tomato paste, salt and cornflour until smooth, then mix into the mushrooms. Bring to the boil, then simmer, covered, over low heat for about 10 minutes until thick and creamy. Stir in the salmon and heat through. Cook the pasta while the sauce is simmering, then drain and place in a large, heated serving dish. Pour the sauce over the top, toss until combined, and serve immediately with a dressed salad, passing a pepper mill at the table. **Serves 6.**

Pesto Pasta with Roasted Tomatoes & Butternut

This pasta dish is a real treat. Only a few ingredients required, and little effort involved, but the result is brilliantly flavoured, colourful, and quite different from most pasta and veg combinations.

500 g Roma tomatoes, quartered*

500 g peeled and cubed butternut (prepared weight)

45 ml (3 Tbsp) olive oil

5 ml (1 tsp) dried oregano

5 ml (1 tsp) sea salt

a sprinkling of light brown sugar

200–250 g fusilli tricolore or pasta screws

about 100 ml (⅖ cup) walnut pesto, or to taste**

shaved pecorino or parmesan and toasted pine nuts for serving

Place the tomatoes and butternut in a baking dish large enough to hold them in a single layer – 32 x 25 x 6 cm is just right. Moisten them with the olive oil, and sprinkle with the oregano, salt and sugar. Roast at 200 °C for about 30 minutes – the tomatoes should be wrinkled and the butternut soft. Meanwhile, cook the pasta, drain well, mix in the pesto, then tip into the roasted vegetables in the baking dish and combine everything gently. Top each serving with shaved pecorino cheese and roasted pine nuts, and if you pass a flat bread and some olive oil for dipping, you'll have a hugely satisfying meal. I also add a bowl of undressed salad leaves – the crunchy freshness is welcome, as the rest of the meal is very generous with oil.

Serves 4–6, depending on the amount of pasta and pesto you wish to use.

* This variety of plum tomato has a deep red colour and is the size and shape of a hen's egg.
** See page 27, or use your favourite pesto.

Saucy Pasta in a Bowl

There are times when you have a craving for pasta but you have *done* pasta with pesto, pasta with olives, pasta with garlic and oil and herbs so often that you can taste everything in your head without going near the kitchen. There are times when you just want to put everything into a pot and go away. That's when this fuss-free dish comes in useful. It's not a mean or a lean meal – it can't be, seeing it requires pecorino and pine nuts – but the chunky vegetable sauce is a simple doddle.

500 g brown mushrooms, wiped and chunkily chopped

2 onions, finely chopped

4 cloves garlic, crushed

400 g baby marrows, pared and diced

1 large red pepper, seeded, ribs removed, and chopped

250 ml (1 cup) red wine

400 ml (1⅗ cups) vegetable or chicken stock

10 ml (2 tsp) dried oregano

5 ml (1 tsp) sea salt

30 ml (2 Tbsp) each flour and butter

250 g pasta screws, cooked at the last minute

grated pecorino, toasted pine nuts and olive oil to accompany

Put the mushrooms, onions, garlic, baby marrows, red pepper, wine, stock, oregano and salt into a large saucepan. Bring to the boil, then reduce the heat immediately, stir to mix, then cover and simmer very gently for about 30 minutes until the vegetables are soft and mingled into a succulent, dark sauce. Mash the flour and butter to a paste and add it in small pats, stirring – you might not need all of it, it depends on how much of the liquid has simmered away – use just enough to thicken the sauce to just coat the pasta. Serve in deep bowls – first the pasta, then a ladleful of sauce, with the cheese, nuts and olive oil passed separately. The end result is hugely satisfying, so no bread required, but an undressed green salad with rocket is good. **Serves 6.**

Robust Tomato Sauce with Herbs

A simple tomato sauce is the starting point for hundreds of pasta dishes and anyone who loves pasta won't need a recipe for the basic mix of tomatoes, onion, garlic, basil and olive oil. The following recipe, however, takes this mix a step further, with the addition of extra herbs and Italian white beans. Canned tomatoes and dried herbs are often used in these sauces, but fresh ingredients have a very special appeal. I also toss in a few mushrooms because I think they enhance almost everything, and although the result is still a basic tomato sauce, it has a lot more personality and flavour than the simpler version.

45 ml (3 Tbsp) olive oil
1 large onion, finely chopped
3 cloves garlic, crushed
1 small green pepper, seeded, ribs removed, and chopped
500 g ripe, juicy tomatoes, skinned and finely chopped
10 ml (2 tsp) tomato paste
15 ml (1 Tbsp) fresh oregano leaves
15 ml (1 Tbsp) fresh thyme leaves
2 bay leaves
a few tufts of parsley
sea salt, milled black pepper and a pinch of sugar
60 ml (¼ cup) red wine
1 x 400 g can cannellini beans, drained and rinsed*
a few fresh basil leaves, shredded
100 g brown mushrooms, wiped, sliced
slivered black olives
a pat of butter
grated parmesan or pecorino cheese for sprinkling

Heat the oil in a large pan and sauté the onion, garlic and green pepper. Add the tomatoes, tomato paste, herbs (except basil), seasoning and wine. Cover and simmer over very low heat for 30–40 minutes. Stir occasionally and mash up the tomatoes with a wooden spoon. (The pan should be covered or the sauce will thicken too much, and the beans will thicken it even further.) Mix in the beans, basil, mushrooms, olives and butter and simmer, covered, for a further 15 minutes – you will probably need to add a little water or stock to keep it succulent. It's the long, gentle simmer that's important here to mellow the flavours – quick tomato sauces can be very tart. Serve on fettucine and pass the cheese. **Serves 4 very generously.**

* These are white kidney beans, larger than haricots, smaller than butter beans.

Beef Steaks with Red Wine & Mushroom Sauce

Many people like a little something with their steak, and this sauce is for them. Make it while the cooked steaks are settling, then spoon it over, or alongside; the rich red-brown colour and medley of flavours will enhance any cut, but it's specially good with rump or fillet.

oil

top-quality soy sauce

6 portions of fillet, or 4 medium rump steaks

1 large leek, thinly shredded

2 cloves garlic, crushed

125 ml (½ cup) red wine

375 ml (1½ cups) hot beef stock

10 ml (2 tsp) tomato paste

200 g brown mushrooms, wiped and chunkily chopped

extra 15 ml (1 Tbsp) soy sauce

20 ml (4 tsp) flour mashed with 20 ml (4 tsp) butter

about 5 ml (1 tsp) redcurrant jelly

Heat a little oil in a large frying pan, brush the steaks on both sides with a *little* soy sauce (this is optional, but it improves the colour and eliminates the need for salt*) and brown on both sides, turning once only and being careful not to pierce them. (Don't do this over fierce heat or the meat will scorch.) When done to your liking, transfer to a plate and keep warm. Add the leek to the same pan and, when it starts to soften and brown, add the garlic, wine, stock and tomato paste. Allow to bubble over medium heat until slightly reduced and boldly coloured, then add the mushrooms and extra soy sauce. When the mushrooms are softening, stir in the flour-butter paste teaspoon by teaspoon, until the sauce thickens, then add the jelly to gloss it and round out the flavour – if you don't have redcurrant jelly, you could try apple or quince – just a touch of sweetness finishes it off perfectly. Now stir in any juices that have escaped under the waiting steaks, and serve. **Serves 4–6.**

* No salt has been added to the ingredients as – unless using low-salt soy sauce – extra salt should not be necessary.

Fillet of Beef with a Creamy Mustard Sauce

This makes a rather special meal for four without breaking the budget because you don't have to cater for seconds – unlike a roast, seconds just don't seem polite when it comes to steaks. So: just four tournedos – cut thick, but small – first marinated, then cooked in minutes and finally drizzled with the cream sauce that is much lighter than most, and a snap to prepare.

4 x 100 g slices of fillet
a slick of oil for frying
sea salt and milled black pepper

MARINADE
60 ml (¼ cup) red wine
10 ml (2 tsp) balsamic vinegar
10 ml (2 tsp) olive oil
5 ml (1 tsp) finely chopped
rosemary leaves

SAUCE
125 ml (½ cup) reduced fat cream
30 ml (2 Tbsp) sweet sherry
20 ml (4 tsp) Dijon mustard
1 small clove garlic, crushed
2 spring onions, finely chopped

Mix all the ingredients for the marinade in a small, shallow glass or non-metallic dish, add the steaks and refrigerate for 4–6 hours, turning a few times. Return the steaks to room temperature before cooking. Take them straight out of the marinade without patting them dry, and use a fairly small frying pan – the steaks should not be crowded, but a large pan will reduce the sauce too much. Heat a little oil and brown the steaks on both sides – turn only once and don't have the heat too fierce or the vinegar will scorch. When done to your liking, transfer to a serving platter, season lightly and keep warm while you make the sauce. Stir all the sauce ingredients together, pour into the same pan in which you cooked the steaks, and stir over low heat until smooth and slightly thickened. Mix in any juices that have accumulated under the waiting steaks, drizzle the steaks with the sauce, and serve at once. **Serves 4.**

Casserole of Veal with Brinjals & Olives

Not unlike the well-loved Osso Buco, but with chunky Mediterranean vegetables adding their individual character and flavour.

1 kg veal shin, in 2 cm thick slices (10–12 slices)
seasoned flour
olive oil
1 x 400 g can whole tomatoes, chopped, plus juice
2 medium brinjals (500 g), cubed and dégorged
3 sticks celery, chopped
12 pickling onions, peeled
15 ml (1 Tbsp) tomato paste
7 ml (1½ tsp) dried tarragon
125 ml (½ cup) white wine
250 ml (1 cup) chicken stock
5 ml (1 tsp) sea salt
10 ml (2 tsp) sugar
6 cloves garlic, peeled
3 bay leaves
black olives (as many as you like)
chopped fresh tarragon or flat-leaf parsley to garnish

Nick the edges of the veal slices, roll in seasoned flour, and brown on both sides in a little olive oil in a frying pan – do this in batches – then arrange in a large baking dish in a single layer. Add the remaining ingredients, except the olives and garnish, to the pan, stir to mix, then cover and simmer for 10 minutes. Pour the sauce over the veal, pushing the onions in between the slices, then cover securely with a lid or a sheet of grease-proof paper and then one of foil, and bake at 160 C for 1 ½ hours, by which time the veal should be butter-soft, the vegetables cooked, and the sauce rich and thick. Stir in the olives and, if necessary, a little extra stock and return to the oven, uncovered, until bubbling. Remove and discard the bay leaves and sprinkle with the tarragon or parsley. **Serves 6.**

Casserole of Lamb with Mushrooms & Butter Beans

An earthy stew, brimming with tender nuggets of lamb and vegetables in a thick, herby gravy. Preparation is surprisingly quick, the baking very slow, and interference from the cook virtually nil, yet the result is simply delicious.

1.1 kg lamb knuckles (20–24), sliced 3–4 cm thick*

seasoned flour

oil

4 cloves garlic, chopped

2 large onions, coarsely chopped

3 medium carrots, sliced

5 ml (1 tsp) each dried thyme and oregano

125 ml (½ cup) red wine

200 ml (⅘ cup) beef stock

200 ml (⅘ cup) tomato puré

125 ml (½ cup) parsley tufts

10 ml (2 tsp) Worcestershire sauce

5 ml (1 tsp) sea salt

10 ml (2 tsp) soft brown sugar

200 g brown mushrooms, wiped and chopped

4 bay leaves

1 x 410 g can butter beans, drained and rinsed

Roll the knuckles in the seasoned flour or shake up in a bag – the easiest way. Brown in batches on both sides in a little oil, then transfer to a large baking dish – 20 x 30 cm is perfect. Place the remaining ingredients, except the mushrooms, bay leaves and beans, in a processor fitted with the metal blade and pulse until the vegetables are finely chopped. Mix with the mushrooms, then spread the mixture over the knuckles. Tuck in the bay leaves and cover securely with a lid, or a sheet of greaseproof paper and then one of foil. Bake at 160 C for 1 hour, then turn and toss the knuckles – the juices will have drawn, but the meat will not yet be tender, and the flavour of the sauce will not have mellowed. Cover as before, and bake for a further 1 hour, then add the beans and bake uncovered for about 15 minutes or until the sauce has thickened sufficiently. Remove and discard the bay leaves and serve piping hot. **Serves 6.**

* **Do not substitute 'stewing' lamb as it is much too fatty.**

Lamb Buffalo with Peppadews

You may wonder about the word 'buffalo' in a recipe without buffalo, but the reason is that the word also features in a chicken dish – also without buffalo, but with a signature tomatoey/ mustardy/sweetish sauce. I can't imagine what a buffalo has to do with such ingredients, but I thought if chicken can respond to it, so can lamb. So here it is: lamb chops slowly simmered until tender in a bright, savoury sauce, spiked with peppadews for oomph. Lovely comfort food, this, for which you will need a really large, heavy, wide-based pan.

30 ml (2 Tbsp) oil and a pat of butter

6 lamb chump chops (about 600 g), trimmed of rind and excess fat

a little sea salt and milled black pepper

1 large onion, sliced into thin rings

2 medium carrots, diced

30 ml (2 Tbsp) flour

125 ml (½ cup) tomato puré

125 ml (½ cup) red wine

250 ml (2 cups) beef stock

10 ml (2 tsp) Worcestershire sauce

30 ml (2 Tbsp) chutney

15 ml (1 Tbsp) wholegrain mustard

2–3 bay leaves

15 ml (1 Tbsp) soft brown sugar

5 ml (1 tsp) mixed dried herbs

a jar of mild sweet piquanté peppers

a handful of chopped flat-leaf parsley or fresh coriander leaves

Heat the oil and butter, brown both sides of the chops, set aside, and season. Add the onion and the carrots to the pan drippings and, when softening, sprinkle in the flour. When absorbed, add all the remaining ingredients, except the peppadews and parsley, in the order listed, stir to mix, then return the lamb to the pan. Cover and simmer gently over very low heat, stirring occasionally, for about 1 hour, turning once, and adding a little extra stock only if necessary. When the chops are very tender and the sauce bright and medium-thick, reach for the jar of peppadews and rinse and chop enough to provide 60–75 ml (4–5 Tbsp). Stir them into the sauce, heat for 10 minutes or so to bring out the flavour, remove the bay leaves, then swirl in the parsley or coriander for colour. Serve on rice or, if your pan is big enough, add a few baby potatoes to cook through just before the chops are tender. **Serves 4–6, with a green veg.**

Braised Leg of Lamb

A pot-roasted or braised leg can never have quite the presence that surrounds a roast, but it nevertheless has a yeoman personality of its own. It is also unfailingly succulent and tender, simple and trustworthy. I love it, and I don't mind that it isn't pink. Also, it's a cook's dream – simply left to languish in the oven for hours along with plenty of wine, stock, vegetables and other things, it emerges butter-soft and afloat with flavour. Add some potatoes before the end, and bake some butternut seeing the oven is on. Two imperatives – you'll need a heavy, lidded roaster that can be used on the stove as well as in the oven – and a *good* red wine.

1.5 kg leg of lamb (without the shank bone)
vinegar
lots of garlic, slivered
15 ml (1 Tbsp) flour mixed with 5 ml (1 tsp) sea salt
about 30 ml (2 Tbsp) oil (and a dab of butter for flavour)
2 large onions, chopped
2 large carrots, diced
1 stick celery, plus leaves, chopped
2 ml (½ tsp) dried oregano
200 ml (⅘ cup) red wine – preferably claret
200 ml (⅘ cup) hot beef stock
2–3 x 10 cm sprigs fresh rosemary
15 ml (1 Tbsp) tomato paste
15 ml (1 Tbsp) soft brown sugar
10 ml (2 tsp) Worcestershire sauce
3 bay leaves

Wipe the leg with vinegar, jab little slits here and there, insert the garlic, and rub all over with the seasoned flour. Heat the oil and butter in the roaster (no rack required with this recipe), brown the lamb on both sides, then remove. Add all the vegetables and the oregano to the drippings in the roaster and sweat briefly over low heat. Return the meat to the roaster, add the remaining ingredients, baste the leg once or twice and then place in the oven at 160 C for 1 ½ hours. Turn the leg, cover again, and bake for a further 1 hour (remember to slip some potatoes round the meat, if using.) Remove to a warm platter to rest – switch off the oven and leave the lamb there while you see to the gravy, which should be plentiful and richly coloured. Either reduce it on top of the stove, which can be rather dodgy because it concentrates the flavours which may be quite concentrated enough already, or break the rules and use cornflour slaked with a little extra red wine, boil up, and when the consistency is right, remove the bay leaves, pour a little over the waiting lamb, and serve the rest separately. **Serves 6.**

Simmered, Savoury Lamb Loin Chops

To be honest, what the title should read is Lamb with Red Wine, Rosemary and Mushrooms but I ducked it because that combination is so well-known and predictable that I just called it something else. The trouble is, when I'm faced with a loin chop, curled up into a tiny round parcel (noisettes are no longer a regular cut, I am told), well, when I see this lamb chop I can think of nothing but red wine, rosemary and mushrooms. There has to be a reason – and I think it is this: the marriage is so perfect, the balance of flavours so impeccable, why follow a different route? I know one should grill them occasionally, and serve them pink, but then they have to be watched, and done this way the chops come with a dark, rich gravy, flavoursome and glossy, and they more or less do themselves.

1–2 cloves garlic
12 lamb loin chops (1–1.2 kg), rind and excess fat removed
60 ml (¼ cup) oil and a pat of butter
sea salt and milled black pepper
4 large leeks, shredded
180 ml (¾ cup) tomato puré
150 ml (⅝ cup) red wine
500 ml (2 cups) beef stock*
2 small sprigs fresh rosemary, bruised
4 sprigs fresh oregano, bruised
4 bay leaves
15 ml (1 Tbsp) soft brown sugar
300 g mixed mushrooms, wiped and coarsely chopped**
1 ml (¼ tsp) ground cinnamon
10 ml (2 tsp) redcurrant, apple or quince jelly

Halve the cloves of garlic and rub well into the chops on both sides. Heat the oil and butter in a very large, deep frying pan and add the chops, tail ends curled round neatly, and brown on both sides. When you get that lovely braai aroma, remove the chops, season lightly and set aside. Soften the leeks in the pan drippings, then add the remaining ingredients up to, and including, the sugar. Bring to simmering point, stirring, then return the lamb to the pan and add the mushrooms and cinnamon. Reduce the heat, cover and simmer very gently for about 30 minutes, turning once – by this time the chops should be really tender, so remove them to a large serving dish, remove the rosemary and oregano from the sauce and boil rapidly for just a few minutes to reduce. Swirl in the jelly to gloss and after a minute or so pour over the chops and serve. **Serves 6.**

* I use Marmite rather than a cube – it makes a dark, flavoursome stock.

** The choice is flexible – I use a mix of brown, button and baby button.

Orange Pork Chops

Bathed in a savoury orange sauce and then slow-baked until meltingly tender, this dish is hassle free, has lots of character, and is quite voluptuously satisfying. Simple accompaniments like mash and broccoli team up perfectly with these bright, succulent chops.

a dash of oil

6 *large* pork loin chops (about 1 kg), without rind or excess fat

a little sea salt

250 ml (1 cup) fresh orange juice

30 ml (2 Tbsp) soy sauce

30 ml (2 Tbsp) smooth chutney

2 ml (½ tsp) ground cinnamon

a small knob of fresh root ginger, peeled and coarsely grated

5 ml (1 tsp) very finely grated orange rind

10 ml (2 tsp) runny honey

60 ml (4 Tbsp) seedless raisins

30 ml (2 Tbsp) flour

verjuice (optional)

Heat the oil in a large frying pan, add the chops and seal quickly on both sides – do not brown. Transfer to a baking dish to fit fairly closely, and season lightly. Quickly mix the orange juice with the rest of the ingredients, except the flour and the verjuice. Add the flour to the pan drippings and, when absorbed, add the orange juice mixture. Stir while it comes to the boil, then pour over the chops. Cover securely with a sheet of greaseproof paper and then one of foil, and bake at 160 C for 1 hour. Turn the chops, cover again, and bake for a further 15 minutes, by which time they should be wonderfully tender in a toffee-coloured sauce. Taste and, if too sweet for your liking, add a dash of verjuice. **Serves 6.**

Sara

One Saturday morning a notice appeared in the *Corriebush Daily* that caused a flutter amongst the women. They all read it while sipping their early-morning tea in bed, and instinctively knew that they should get up quickly and meet at The Coffee Shop for a round-table discussion. By ten o'clock they were all there – Amelia, Lily, Anna, Sophia, Nellie and Maria. Nellie poured, while Lily passed the scones.

'So what do you think?'

'I think we should all do it.'

'It's not everyday that we get a chance like this.'

'I always knew I had a novel inside me.'

'Me too. Something in the style of Jane Austen, I think.'

'The fees are reasonable, too.'

'What's her name again?'

Anna took the newspaper out of her shopping bag. 'Here it is,' and she read aloud. 'Victoria Abbeyfield, the well-known international author, is touring the country offering creative writing classes in various centres. She will be in Corriebush next week, and anyone who has ever longed to write – be it children's stories, poetry, novels or an autobiography – is welcome to attend. Classes are limited to six, therefore anyone interested should waste no time in enrolling. This can be done at the newspaper office. A small deposit is required.'

Leaving their coffee half-drunk, their scones barely touched, they rushed.

'It's poetry for me,' said Sophia. 'Comes naturally. Like:

The sun by day and the moon by night
They brighten the land with a lovely light.'

'Jolly good Sophia,' they said kindly, and then, having filled in their forms and paid their deposits, went shopping for pencils and notebooks.

The following Monday found them sitting excitedly in the council chamber behind the Town Hall, where the classes were to be held. Victoria Abbeyfield sat at a table in the front. A small, thin lady, wearing horn-rimmed spectacles, her hair pulled into a wispy bun in the nape of her neck, a single string of pearls, a beige twin-set, flat chest. They were a little disappointed.

'I thought she'd look very rich,' Anna whispered to Nellie. 'You know, just like the photographs you see on the back flaps of books – lots of curly hair, big soulful eyes, faces resting in their hands, fingers full of rings.'

'Never mind, with nine best-sellers, two divorces and a third husband under her belt she's probably quite worn out, but she must also be very clever, and that's what counts in this sort of situation.'

And indeed, Victoria was not only clever, she was experienced and patient, and knew just how to set any shred of imagination in motion.

'I want you ladies,' she said, 'to close your eyes and think back to your childhoods. Don't scramble around in your minds, just remember the first thing that comes up. Hold it, and then I want you to tell it. Because that's where I like to start – way down in memory lane. Writing from experience is always the purest form of expression. So just sit back for five minutes, and then I'll ask you what has come to you out of the past. It may be a wonderful surprise, it may be something that frightened you, it may be sad or happy or connected with your parents. Just sit now, and let go.'

For five minutes there was total silence in the room as they sat, each at a table, eyes tight shut, trying to unravel their years.

Maria was the first to open her eyes.

'You see something, Maria? Something spring to mind?'

Maria shuddered. 'It was horrible.' Now they were all awake, sitting up and listening. 'I was ten years old and it was the night before the school bazaar. We had to get there very early to set up the tables, so I put my gym tunic, shirt and tie over the chair in my room, all ready, in order to save time in the morning. It was still half-dark when I jumped out of bed, pulled on my shirt and tunic and then reached for my 'tie'. Half-way to slinging it round my neck, I knew. It was not a tie. It was a snake.'

The women gasped and shook their shoulders in little wobbles of horror. 'I screamed and flung it across the room and my father rushed in and killed it. It's true.'

'My goodness,' commented Victoria. 'I don't quite see a full story there, but hang onto it, we might be able to develop it into Tales of the South African Veld, or something like that.'

Sophia was wriggling in her chair, eager for her turn. 'What came into my head was also about school. When I threw my teacher with a pomegranate.' 'We'll correct the grammar later,' said Victoria. 'But please carry on, Sophia.'

'It was the first day of term and we had a new teacher, and so she had to go round the classroom asking for all our full names and surnames, and when it was my turn, she put her hands over her face and laughed and laughed. I knew, because her shoulders were shaking like a jelly and she was making little snorting noises, and tears were running out between her fingers and …'

'But what did you tell her that caused all this? What *is* your full name then?'

'Sophia.'

'Go on.'

'Sophia Aspidistra.'

Victoria's face remained impassive. 'Well, that certainly is an unusual name, Sophia, but there was no need for her to be so rude.'

'No, no need at all. So I took out my lunchbox. My mother had given me two mutton sandwiches and a pomegranate – we had a long pomegranate hedge in our garden – and I took it out and threw her with it.'

'Threw it *at* her, Sophia.'

'No, I walked up to her and threw it, hard, on the top of her head. I used both hands, and she went 'hic', like that, and the red pips spattered all over the floor, and then she turned pale and fell over.'

'Oh dear, Sophia. What then?'

'Well, Hettie, who sat next to me, went to call the headmistress and she helped the teacher out – took her by the arm and supported her to the staffroom and – do you know what – she never came back!'

'Well now. It would be difficult to turn that into a full-length story, Sophia, but not impossible. One would have to put a moral in it somewhere. Perhaps you could meet her some years later – let's make it at the seaside. You're both swimming and she is suddenly knocked over by a wave, you save her from drowning, and then you both forgive each other and become friends. *Aspidistra To the Rescue – A Story For Young People.* How does that sound to you?'

'Like *blerrie* nonsense,' answered Sophia under her breath, while she nodded and smiled sweetly at Victoria.

Victoria turned to Anna.

'Not ready yet.'

'Nellie?'

'Thinking, thinking …'

'Amelia?'

'Just a few more minutes.'

'Your turn then, Lily.'

Lily was sitting very, very still.

'Lily, it's your turn now!'

Lily seemed not to have heard Victoria, but to have gone somewhere else, into a space deep inside. Her eyes were staring at nothing, unblinking and clouded.

'Lily?'

And then, in a voice almost as soft as a whisper, Lily started.

'The story is not mine. It was told to me by my mother, who was told it by her mother, who heard it from *her* mother. It is about a child called Sara Liebenberg, who was one of our family a very long time ago.' A long pause. 'I asked my mother to write it all down in a book, and I read it so often I think I know it by heart, word for word as the story was passed down.'

'Go on then, Lily.'

'It's a very long story, do you mind?'

'Of course not. Carry on.'

'It was a bitterly cold evening. As we all know, summer days here in the Karoo are so hot that the veld trembles with heat; mirages melt the scorched kopjes and the bushes shrivel to spiky scrunches in just a few hours. The birds don't sing, they are nowhere; even the cicadas are quiet as the world seems to stop, only waking again at sunset. But the winters are different. Especially the nights, when the veld lies stretched out taut, cracked with frost under a frozen white moon. People hesitate to go outside, for it is a dry, aching cold and the air makes them gasp.

'My story starts on such a winter's night. It was July 1835.

'Inside the small, white-washed farmhouse Sara lay snuggled under a pile of feather blankets in a four-poster bed. Beside her, her sister and small brother, Anna Maria and Christiaan, lay sleeping soundly, but Sara was wide awake, disturbed by strange noises coming from the *voorkamer*. Not the usual, homely sounds to which she was accustomed – coffee bubbling in the old brass urn, the servants singing psalms round the fire, her papa tapping his pipe on the hearth – but the frightening rasp of a man's voice raised in anger.

'Quietly Sara crept out of bed and tip-toed through to the *voorkamer*, where she stood in the doorway; a fair-haired little girl of nine, in a long white nightdress flecked with shadow and firelight. They were sitting round the dining room table; her father, her mother, and a stranger – a man with a thick black beard hanging down over his knotted neck cloth – and he was shouting, banging his fist on the table until the crockery rattled. 'I tell you, Barend! I tell you now as surely as I am sitting here and my name is Pieter Kruger, I tell you that there is only one – *only one* – answer to the problems that we Boer farmers face. WE HAVE TO TREK!'

'Sara's mother, Estella, looked up sharply. 'You mean we should leave Olyffontein, Piet? Move again? Haven't we trekked often enough?'

'I know, I know, Estella,' Pieter addressed her more soothingly. 'It's hard, but it's the only way. We *have* to get away from this *verdomde* British government, and the only way we can do it is to trek away from the Colony. Go north! They say there's wonderful country beyond these borders – open, empty land, good grazing, and *freedom*.'

Then he turned back to Barend and, holding up his hand, ticked off his grievances one by one. 'Now listen here man. First, there's the question of security. Bah! What security?

We will *never* have security under this government! There's no law and order and there's no protection. There's no fair judicial system. And there's tribal theft and plunder. Constantly. They set our houses on fire and drive our cattle away. Then – can you believe it – we are forbidden, *forbidden*, Barend, to take back the stolen stock!'

Barend nodded. 'Yes, it's happened to me too, lost most of my herd, and my house reduced to ashes.'

'Then take the missionaries, Barend – especially that damned Read and Van der Kemp. They run off tattling to England, putting the blame for all the wars and destruction on us, the farmers, and *the government believes them*! Calls us criminals!'

'I know Pieter, I had to travel for days to appear in court, even though I knew that the charges were false! They always believe the missionaries, never the Boers. And of course there's also the slave question, and the financial losses …'

Kruger did not wait for Barend to finish. He was so angry now that he leapt off his chair and banged both fists on the table. Estella jumped with fright. 'That's right! Free The Slaves they say! Set them free and then you – you Boer peasants – you can come to England to fetch your money. And then don't expect much!' He slammed the table. 'NO, NO my friends! We cannot live any longer under the British flag – especially, *especially* now that Dutch, *our* language, is slowly but surely being replaced by English.'

He was becoming tired now, his head beginning to droop. '*Ag* no. They have taken away our labour, our freedom, our language – and worst of all – our dignity. There is no peace here; only turbulence, and ruin. Barend and Estella, WE HAVE TO GO! Let us trek over the mountains where we can be proud and independent, and start again.'

Nothing more was said. Piet Kruger sat dead still now, staring at the table. Sara's father clasped his huge hands together and bent over them, as though he were praying. His wife quietly went on embroidering the black satin shawl on her lap. The room was alive with emotion.

Finally Estella Liebenberg scraped back her chair. 'Would you like something to drink Pieter?' she asked, measuring some roasted grain into the brass teapot. 'I'm afraid we have no more tea leaves, but we still have some sugar candy,' and she passed a small tin box. 'If you take a sip of this, and then suck some candy, it is not so bitter, and really quite refreshing.'

Sara drew back into the shadows. She knew she would be sent away if they saw her, but how could she leave her father when he looked so upset? Why were his fingers

shaking as he lit his old clay pipe? Sara caught the fragrant smell of the tobacco with which he stuffed it. The tobacco hung in long thick ropes from the rafters under the thatch, together with the mealie cobs and the carcasses of freshly killed sheep. Glancing up, she could just see the coils hanging there like looped snakes, first black, then copper-red as the flames in the open hearth licked up and down the walls. Between the coils of tobacco hung her father's hunting equipment and his sjamboks of rhino hide, strings of calabashes, and dried fruit. The floor on which Sara stood was made of antheaps, first pounded into dust and then watered and stamped. It was hard and cool, and her feet were beginning to feel cold. She crept back to the bedroom. She would tell Anna Maria and Christiaan in the morning.

Piet Kruger did not spend the night. He needed to get home, he said, his wife and children were alone and he felt uneasy about leaving them. After he had left, galloping on his horse into the freezing night, the Liebenbergs did not go to bed. They sat, instead, next to the fire in the kitchen while Barend spoke gently to his wife about his decision.

'Remember when I went to *Nagmaal* last month?' Estella nodded. Normally the whole family would have gone, but she was pregnant with their fourth child and the journey to Colesberg – twelve days by ox wagon – would have been too much of a risk. 'Well, the evening before the church service, we were called to a meeting in the town square. We were addressed by Sarel Cilliers – I remember him so well: a short, stocky man, with long sideburns and a fair beard, wearing knee breeches and a frock coat. He stood on a chair in the middle of us all, and this is what he said:

"Brethren," he began, "the time has come for the Afrikaner nation to rise up and go. We are a peace-loving and God-fearing people. And this is our country. We have no ties with any other home. We were born here, and wish to remain here, sons of the soil. We have pioneered the land, paid our taxes and done military service. In return we expect justice and security. And what do we get, brethren? *What do we get?*"

'And they told him. Emotionally, passionately they told him; standing there in the light of the fire, holding their hats in their hands. Stories of hardship and loss, poverty and war. And after the last man had spoken, Cilliers stood again on his chair. "We do not know what lies ahead, brethren, but we do know that here, in the Colony, we farmers stand alone and unsupported. Every nation has its faults, and the British government does have many good intentions and many noble and honourable men in its service, but they will *never* understand us and our problems, because they're too far away. To the north of this country we hope to find our freedom; no laws, no wars, we can build other farms, new lives … Brethren, we must rise up and go." Then he held up his hand. "But remember! We go in peace. We wish to harm no man."'

'We must leave Olyffontein, Estella.' His wife bent her head and nodded. She was used to moving. This would be the fifth time.

Preparations started early next morning, as bit by bit their home was taken apart and packed away into three canvas-covered wagons which could be dismantled for floating across rivers or descending steep slopes. Their clothes were packed into chests – parasols and muffs in one, everyday wear in the others – bonnets, chintz dresses, flap-trousers, *velskoene* and linen shirts. Onto the main wagon went a large wooden *katel* strung

together with *riempies*, while the others carried the four-poster beds, the stinkwood settee, the copper moulds and pewter tureens. The three-legged iron cooking pots were hooked on the outside, with space for crates of fowls in between.

'Can I take my dolls, Papa?' asked Sara, looking for a chest into which she could stuff them. 'We'll take as much as we can, Saratjie,' he replied, putting his arm round her shoulders, 'so that we can start our new life in comfort, surrounded by our beloved old possessions. We're going to have a fine home again, my treasure. A big farm, somewhere in the north, with running streams and waving grass, soft blue mountains and every kind of animal you can imagine.'

Estella worked from before dawn until late at night, baking *beskuit*, preparing biltong with salt and coriander, filling bins with meal for bread, making candles and soap with sheeptail fat and woodash and soda. She and the children filled bags with seeds so that they could plant again, as soon as they were settled – mealies and oats and fertile plum pips, apricots and peaches. And then they sewed twelve spare bonnets, *kappies*, for the sun.

The family left on the 2nd of January, 1836. The three wagons with Estella and the children and their faithful servants Gawie and Antjie, with their sons to act as *voorloopers*. Barend rode ahead on his horse, threading a path between the large bushes and watching for anthills.

Sara looked back. The house seemed very small, very lonely, and even as she looked, the heatwaves shimmered over the walls, stifling the house and trees in a pale, blistering haze. Sadly, she turned and looked ahead. To the right, to the left, all around there lay nothing but the endless, rippling, copper-hot Karoo.

Their *trekkie* was but one of many. In the New Year of 1836, there were sixty wagons, white-canopied and gaily painted, threading their way across the plains to Colesberg. Day after day the oxen plodded on in the swirling dust, and day after day the sun rose triumphantly, splashing the east with volcanic colour. Anxiously they scanned the skies for signs of rain, while the cicadas laughed and thrummed out their brittle chorus and the heat hung, thick and turgid, over the aching countryside. They could not travel at the height of day. By five o'clock in the morning they had inspanned and moved off. At eleven, they stopped again, and then at four, when the cool west wind, the *droogtewindjie* sprang up, they moved on until sunset, when they outspanned for the night.

Like several other families, the Liebenbergs had to spend a few days at Colesberg, waiting for the last members of the party to arrive – Botha, Kruger, Steyn, Brits … And then, with unquestioning faith and the singular determination of the Boer, they gathered their families together and set off north under the leadership of Sarel Cilliers. A band of refugees, so proud, so courageous – and quite desperately naïve and unaware.

Sara was happy. To be continually surrounded by cousins and friends meant games and laughter and lots of fun. Each day was different, shining and new. Always exciting, sometimes frightening, like the morning of the third day, when Sara was woken by a strange noise. It sounded like a roll of thunder, except that it did not swell to a crescendo and die away, it just went on and on: a dull, hollow drumming, a pounding and a rumbling that shook the wagon in which they lay.

'What is it Papa?' Sara sat up wide-eyed, alarmed.

Her father was outside already, staring into the distance.

'Come and see,' he answered.

Far away there was a great mountain of red dust. And the mountain moved, and it was the mountain that made the rumbling noise, and inside the mountain, dimly, through the thick copper of mountain cloud, Sara could see shapes moving. White things that shot this way and that and up and down, now high, now low, furious, faster, stamping and thrumming.

'They are springbok,' her father said. 'A herd of fleeing springbok, and they are very dangerous. Had we been in their path they would have trampled us and the oxen to death; cut us to pieces with their flint-like hooves. We've been lucky.'

'But why are they running, Papa? Why are they storming so, instead of jumping one by one, here and there, like we always see at home?'

'Because they are very, very thirsty, Sara, and they smell water. And nothing will stop them from getting to the water. If we travelled behind them we would find dead wildebeest, blesbok, eland, zebras, all kinds of animals lying trampled and torn. And inside that bunch they could be carrying along lions and leopards, all crushed up amongst them.'

Now the drumming grew fainter; the red cloud shrank, bounced over the horizon, and disappeared.

Gradually the pattern of the days established itself. Up at dawn, a *skof* of several miles, a rest during the midday heat, when most people retired to the wagons and slept. Everyone was tired. Because there were not many servants, the children frequently had to drive the sheep, herding them over the brittle, bumpy veld. Often long mimosa thorns would pierce their soft leather shoes, the scraggly bushes reaching out and tearing their long skirts, while their mothers sat on the chests on the fronts of the wagons with their babies on their laps and drove the oxen.

Sometimes Barend would come riding up to their wagon, carrying a terrible yellow or black snake by the tail, its head clubbed to a pulp, its body still throwing coils in the air. Sometimes he would point out a pride of lions sleeping under a clump of thorn trees, or a herd of zebras, fat and shiny, galloping in the distance, or ostriches giant-striding over the bushes, with their bobbing necks and flapping wings. But the fearsome ones were the lynxes and hyaenas and leopards, which would slink into the sheep enclosures at night, rip open their stomachs and leave entrails and blood all over.

Sara's great friend was her cousin, Laetitia Steyn. During the day they were seldom apart and were usually to be found sitting at the back of one of the wagons, bare feet dangling, skirts billowing, sharing secrets, dried peaches, and *vetkoek* with dripping.

'They say *Tant* Lettie Brits had her baby kneeling behind the wagon,' Laetitia told her friend. 'And it came out with the cord wound four times round its neck. My mother says *Tant* Lettie's as strong as an ox. Two days later she was leading the span, baby in one hand, *riem* in the other.'

'Well,' Sara countered, 'Antjie told me that her mother had eleven children, and that they used to just drop like plums, she said, while she was herding the sheep, and she'd pick them up and walk home at the end of the day. She'd set off in the morning with just the dog and the sheep and come back with a baby every year, eleven times.'

Sara loved the evenings on trek. They always started with a sudden whoosh of whiplashes, and voices calling to voorlopers and beasts to halt. This meant that they had found a suitable spot for the night. Sometimes it was next to a dam. Usually there was thick green slime quilting the surface of the water, bubbling and sucking as the wind drove it from one side to another. But it was water, nevertheless, with clear pools here and there in which to wash their clothes before spreading them out on the bushes to dry. Now, too, her mother would remove her goatskin mask. How Sara hated it! 'Have you noticed how funny she looks?' she asked Laetitia. 'I get so ashamed. But she says the most important thing about a woman's face is her skin. She doesn't want to look like a ploughed furrow when we get to our new farm.'

While the women washed clothes and prepared the evening meal – often venison steak with stewed pumpkin and boiled corn, the men would construct the thorn bush enclosures for the animals, and then sit sipping their special coffee – *boeretroost* they called it, which the women brewed in kettles hanging from tripods over the fires.

Then the prayers. Usually late, Sara and Laetitia would run to join the group standing round the fires, prayer book in hand. Psalms, the Lord's prayer, a short sermon. The firelight would flicker over the upturned faces. Round them the veld would be carpeted black, the thorn trees standing still, not moving, listening. Only the owls in the branches

would stir, as the moon rose over the strange assembly. Round the fires they would stand, the men holding their hats in their hands, bearded and dusty. And their women, still wearing their bonnets, their *kappies*, would sing with their children on their hips or asleep on their shoulders. The voices, deep bass, sweet treble, hung on the thick night air. Even the animals were still. In the end there was no sound but the voice reading from the scriptures; no movement but the flames gently dying in the spent fires; no brightness but what shone in their eyes. The trekker's religion was the most important influence in his life.

One evening, after the last Amen had been said, Sarel Cilliers walked to the centre of the gathering. 'I have had word,' he told them, 'that Andries Hendrik Potgieter – who, as you know, has been trekking just ahead of us, has now crossed the Orange River. He has sent a messenger to tell us that it is in full flood, but that they managed by floating the wagons across on rafts.' A ripple ran through the listeners. They knew that the river was very close now, that the problem would soon be theirs. 'With the help of God we shall get across in the same way,' he went on, his fair hair touched red by the light from the embers. 'At a point beyond the river, the Blesberg, he will wait for us.'

Now they murmured excitedly; at last there was a hint of the real freedom they sought; that distant, Promised Land was soon to become a reality. And they would feel safer, linking up with Potgieter and his bigger party. That night they went to bed with light hearts. What did it matter that a mere ribbon of water lay ahead of them? Beyond it was their destiny. Just a few more months and they would be able to settle down and start again.

Next day the men galloped ahead to check the level of the water in the river. When they reached the bank, no-one said a word, did not shout, nor exclaim. They simply reined in their horses and gazed in shocked silence. Before them tumbled a twisting, heaving sea of dark water. A great chocolate snake it was, gliding furiously, bubbling and sucking, up and down, round and round, roaring its tumultuous way to the sea. Black with mud, heavy with logs and branches and dead cows, it was a terrifying sight.

'We'll have to wait until the river drops,' someone eventually shouted above the roar of the water.

'Don't talk nonsense, man! It could be weeks! We'll make a plan.'

When the rest of the party arrived, Sara gazed at the heaving water and felt sick with fear. 'Papa, what will we do? I'm so frightened.'

'We'll do nothing that will harm a hair on your head, my heart,' he comforted her. 'We'll find a narrow place where the animals can swim across. Then we'll turn the wagons into boats, and sail you over! Won't that be fun?'

All that day, and the next, they worked, chopping down willow trees that lined the banks, lashing the branches together with strong *riems*. Then they removed the wheels, and sat the bodies of each wagon on a raft. The first family climbed aboard and were poled across the river. One by one they followed, the small children crying out in terror, the men shouting instructions, the water slapping hard against the logs. The women sat with their children round their skirts and sang hymns. They sang to hide their fear, holding up their psalm books so as not to see the gushing water. They sang to avoid thinking about what would happen if the raft split and the wagon sank slowly into that cold, rushing river.

And when they reached the other side and stepped onto the wet, safe ground, they went down on their knees and thanked God. 'At last we are free!' and they looked around at the flat blue *koppies* fading into the distance. 'We are free.' Some wept.

Progress was fairly slow through the Griqua territory – a friendly, intelligent people who could ride horses and handle guns as well as any of them. They were the first of several tribes the trekkers would come across, the friendliest being the smiling Basutos, who hurried along with beans and corn and mealies in exchange for Boer cattle and sheep. Sara's mother was overjoyed, for their supplies had run very low.

'Bean soup and mealie porridge tonight! *Ag* what a feast!'

Hendrik Potgieter and his trek were waiting for them at the Blesberg, near the kraal of Moroka, chief of the Barolongs at Thaba Nchu on the Basuto border. With both parties having managed to cross the river, the meeting was a particularly joyous one. Potgieter was an impressive man, very tall, obstinate, fiercely independent and a natural leader.

'The old blue one,' the children called him, for he had piercing blue eyes and wore a blue moleskin Dopper jacket. He was immediately elected commandant and Trek ruler.

For a week they rested where they were. The women needed to mend clothes, make butter from sheep tail fat, and replenish their supplies of soap and candles, while the men had to attend to the wagons, repair broken *disselbooms* and damaged axles, yoke straps and drag ropes. Sick animals needed attention, and *riems* had to be greased. On the eighth day they started off once more, keeping to the east, trundling confidently through the lush green lowveld grass.

Before long, however, Potgieter announced that they had completed the first stage of their journey.

'Here you must stay,' he told them. 'Camp out, make a home, while I go north to the Vaal River and beyond, to look for other treks and to see the country. I *beg* you, *command* you to remain here, for we know nothing of what lies beyond and it will be safer if you all stay together.'

And for some months they did. The stock grew fat, the banks of the river ran with game, the children were happy, strong and healthy. But, unfortunately, it was not in the nature of the Trekboer to outspan for too long. Having come so far, the sudden restriction of staying in one place while waiting for permission to move on, became unacceptable. The spirit of adventure simmered steadily and they simply had to go forward, had to keep moving. One by one, they wandered off to the north.

It was then that Barend Liebenberg made the most devastating decision of his life. 'Let us also move forward slowly,' he told his family one morning. 'It is too difficult to sit still here, waiting, waiting; we won't go too far.' When they reached the Vaal River they forded it where it ran low, and then they stopped. 'Far enough,' Barend said.

So they camped out. It was early spring, the sun was warmer, the grass, the trees, were mint-green new. The river filled and swelled, fed by the springs in the mountains. Flowers bloomed between the bushes; birds nested in the trees along the banks; the whole world was thawing and bursting into life. There was no hint of the horror that was about to swamp them.

The date was August 24th, l836.

Mzilikazi sat outside the royal lodge at eGabeni.

It was early in the day, and a pale spring sun shone through the wild olive branches. In the fields the cows were being milked, lowing gently as the young herdboys tugged at their udders. From the royal harem came the soft sound of voices humming; the shuffling of bare feet on baked earth.

A young girl emerged and came slowly towards him, her oiled skin shining like that of a sleek wet seal. A short ox-hide skirt covered her loins, and round her neck and her waist hung necklaces of shining beads. Like his other wives, she kept her head shaved except for a small tuft on the top, and this, too, was threaded with a network of bright beads. As she neared the king, she sank to her knees and crept forward slowly, balancing an earthenware pot of beer on her head. Sour beer, made from millet, it was the red-brown colour of a mountain stream after rain. Lifting the pot carefully, she placed it before her handsome master, and then shuffled backwards, never turning her back on him, hardly daring to look.

Mzilikazi grunted. He was in no mood for women this morning. Recent reports from his *indunas* had disturbed him and he had lain awake all night, trying to decide on a course of action. Finally he decided to send for his councillors and military commanders, Mkalipi and Marapu, Kampa and Sibekhu, to discuss the matter.

Mzilikazi sat and waited. The sun was climbing high; his fat-smeared limbs shone red-black and glistening. He was of stocky but muscular build, only slightly rotund, and very powerful. On his head he wore an otter skin stuffed and rolled into a tight circle, and stuck with bunches of blue jay feathers. In the centre front waved a white ostrich feather, the insignia of royalty. Round his neck were hung strings of coloured beads and his loins were covered with clusters of monkey tails.

At last his men arrived and, led by Mkalipi, advanced on their knees. 'Bayete!' they shouted. 'Bayete! King of Kings! Great Bull Elephant!' Motioning them to sit down, their king covered his steaming shoulders with his favourite giraffe skin, took a long draught of beer, and spoke. His voice was soft, high-pitched and melodious.

'I am told that strangers have entered our territory from the south, without permission.' An angry murmur broke out among the councillors. 'Not Griquas this time, with their yellow faces; nor Korannas on their fast brown cows without horns; not missionaries like my friend Moffat, nor hunters like the man Bain. But people in moving houses they call wagons, with their cattle and sheep and guns.'

Anxiously they glanced at each other. Like their king, they were suspicious of strangers. If they came in peaceful, small groups and asked his permission, he seldom refused and allowed them to hunt game. But they knew that the only way he could remain sovereign over all his territory was to be ready to kill anyone who entered it without his consent. For this reason, Mkalipi's duty was to patrol the southern boundary of the Matabele kingdom, the area along the Vaal River, to watch for any trespassers coming up from the south. And now this had happened! People had crossed the river. And the Matabele were afraid.

With a sudden sweep of his arm, the king knocked over the pot of beer. It spread in a stain over the dusty soil; made rivulets in the sand and oozed under his feet. 'Will we, the Matabele, allow strangers to come into our midst like snakes in the night?' he shouted. 'Have they my permission? What are they seeking?'

He was trembling now, with anger and fear, and his councillors, sensing his mood, leapt to their feet. One by one they walked back and forth, shouting their opinions, striking the ground with their sticks, becoming angrier and angrier, stamping their feet on the ground and leaping into the air in a frenzied dance of fury.

For a while the king watched, sipping his beer, now and then dipping into a large basket of fresh, fatty meat. Then he called for silence and, taking his cloak, laid it on the

ground. 'That cloak,' he said, pointing, 'belongs to Mzilikazi, king of the country from the Lebombo Mountains to the Drakensberg! I am Mzilikazi, the Great Bull Elephant! No-one will touch me!'

'Bayete! Bayete!' the councillors shouted in chorus, bowing their heads in worship.

And as they sat there in the hot noonday sun in the enormous royal kraal at eGabeni, within the circles of perfect, beehive-shaped huts inside the thick thorn-tree hedge, their king told them, once again, his story.

In Zululand, between the Sikwebezi and Mkuze rivers, lived the Khumalo clan. There were three chiefs altogether; Mashobane was chief of the north. He chose his wife, Nompethu, from the Ndwandwe tribe and when she bore him a son, they named him Mzilikazi, which means The Great Road. Being the heir to the throne, this was an important child, and so he was sent to be educated at the royal kraal of his grand-father, Zwide.

It was in this verdant country that Mzilikazi grew to manhood. Cared for by both his mother and the gentle young girls in the royal kraal, his childhood was sheltered and happy. When he was just five years old, he was put in charge of a small group of calves, and then, at the age of twelve, he joined the older boys who looked after the royal cattle. It was from these boys that the future king learnt almost everything that a young Zulu needed to know. He learnt that cattle were the most important possessions in a ruler's life because the power of a chief, and the wealth of his people, depended solely on the number of livestock he owned. He learned that they were killed for sacrificial rites, rarely for eating; that they provided the tribe with sour milk; and that their dung was good for plastering floors and grain pits. And the young Mzilikazi developed a passion for acquiring cattle that was to last him all his life.

During those long days in the open veld he learnt the rudiments of self-protection. Soon he knew which plants and berries were safe to eat, and which would kill both cattle and man. He learnt which animals and spiders to fear, and which were harmless; how to kill a small buck with a swiftly aimed stone; to trap guinea fowl and wring their necks; to pulp the head of a deadly snake in an instant. Armed with nothing but a shield and a spear, he had to prove himself a match for wild dogs and leopards. From the older boys

he learnt about women and their delights, but also that they would be forbidden fruit for years to come. First, on reaching manhood, he had to undergo the strict military training to which all youths were subjected. Strong armies were essential at this time, for Zululand was beginning to swell and heave with political unrest like a troubled sea, and all tribes and clans were uneasy and preparing for strife.

The bubbling pot of dissension boiled most fiercely south of the Black Mfolozi, among the Mthethwa peoples. Their chief, Dingiswayo, was an ambitious ruler, determined to shape his people into the most powerful tribe in the country and a young man, Shaka – a fearless and cunning fighter – was installed as leader of the army, and later as Zulu chief. From his royal kraal, Bulawayo, he trained his warriors to fight to the death. When Mzilikazi's father died – he was, in fact, murdered – Mzilikazi did not return to his home to take his place as the new chief. He knew of Shaka, realised that this chief was destined to become all-powerful, and so rather than suffer defeat at Shaka's hands, he decided to join him. And so Mzilikazi and his Khumalo clan trekked to Bulawayo.

Shaka was pleased. The Khumalo brought with them their cattle and their warriors and their promising young chief. In time Mzilikazi and Shaka became good friends. Mzilikazi proved to be a brilliant leader and fearless fighter, and Shaka appointed him commander-in-chief of the army he was mustering to attack a Sotho tribe. It was fortunate that Shaka favoured Mzilikazi, for he was an excessively cruel chief, and anyone who displeased him was shown no mercy. Torture and bloodshed, mass murders, live burial and impalement were common at Gibixhegu, Shaka's new kraal.

And then this same bloody fate almost befell Mzilikazi. He grew tired of being subservient to Shaka. 'It was *I* who defeated the Sotho and captured their cattle, so why should I not keep them?' he reasoned. 'Why must I give everything I fight for to Shaka?' And so he and his warriors drove the cattle to his own kraal, and kept them. Shaka was furious. Immediately he sent a group of envoys to demand that Mzilikazi bring back the cattle, or he would take revenge.

Knowing that Shaka's revenge would be terrible, Mzilikazi mustered his little clan of just 300 warriors and a number of women and children, and fled. 'Let us move far away and establish our own kingdom, where we will be free of Shaka and his wrath. I hear the grazing is good in the north, and I, Mzilikazi, will show you the way.'

And so, in 1823, the Great March started, and the incredible, bloody saga of Mzilikazi and his people, the Matabele, began.

At the start it was a story of one hard battle after another. Mzilikazi's army was small compared to the other clans, but he had the ability to plan and to lead, and such was his charisma that his people followed him like a god. For him, his warriors would destroy themselves without hesitation, and confidently they followed him beyond the Drakensberg and into Sotho territory. The Sotho were a cattle-breeding nation, and their numbers were vast, but Mzilikazi wanted their cattle, and his strategy was lethal.

During the day his scouts would prowl the countryside, establishing the area to be raided. And then, during the night, they would steal silently through the long grass, oval shields in one hand, short stabbing spears in the other. Soundlessly they would encircle the slumbering villages, waiting, until at a given signal they would leap into the air with a terrible shouting and rattling of shields. And as the terrified Sotho ran out of their huts they would butcher them, set fire to the thatch, ransack the entire village and drive the cattle back to their headquarters.

As Mzilikazi became richer and more powerful, he fearlessly led his regiments himself.

Behind him came his warriors in their monkey-tail kilts, clusters of feathers waving on their heads, garters of ox-hair below their knees, carrying their huge shields, assegais, spears and *knobkieries*. And as they conquered one clan after the other the numbers in their army swelled, as the triumphant warriors brought back their captives. Mzilikazi knew that his power was great, but he also knew that he would be in constant danger if he did not increase the numbers of his tribe; it was not only cattle and food and land that a ruler needed, he also needed recruits for his army and women to serve as their concubines. And so the young boys and girls were spared, but the old people and the babies were left to die in their smouldering villages.

Finally Mzilikazi decided that he had put enough distance between him and Shaka, and the time had come to settle. He would have his own royal kraal, an established settlement, where crops could be grown and a harem set up for his entertainment. And so, near the Middelburg (Mpumalanga) of today, close to the upper Olifants River, where the climate was mild and the land rich with game, ekuPhumuleni – the Place of Rest – came into being. For months his people toiled, little domed huts mushroomed, military barracks took shape, and the great royal enclosure was completed.

During this year of 1824, Mzilikazi's star burned ever more brightly. More tribes were conquered, more warriors recruited into his army, and more cattle added to his herds. For a time he and his people lived in plenty. He was the Lion of the Land, the Great Bull Elephant. But then the summer came and even the Great Elephant could not make rain. The sun burnt furiously, day after day, in a cloudless sky. And when their crops shrivelled and died, the scorched fields lay bare and cracked, the cattle lowed pitifully and collapsed at the empty water holes, then Mzilikazi knew that this Place of Rest was, perhaps, not his divine destiny after all. A nation needed food and a king's wealth lay in his cattle. A hungry nation was a dissatisfied nation, and when their bellies were empty, men could not fight.

He sent his spies out to the west. They returned with tales of the wonderful country that lay between the Magaliesberg mountains and the Limpopo. This was the land of the Bakwena – the Crocodile People, whose cattle were fat, and whose cornfields stretched for miles. Here, too, he would be even further away from Shaka, and so, in 1825, at the close of the summer, the second great exodus began. In a solid, rumbling mass they went, a wave of virile but obedient people, led by their king Mzilikazi, The Great Road.

By the time they reached the bushveld, it was too late for the Bakwena to flee. Mzilikazi sent a large regiment to wipe them out, and in a short time the Matabele were stronger and richer than ever.

Close to the junction of the Apies and Crocodile rivers, Mzilikazi started again, and built his next royal kraal, Hlahlandlela.

'I, Mzilikazi, must be the strongest and greatest of them all,' he reasoned 'or I, Mzilikazi, shall die.' You either annihilated your enemies, or were annihilated yourself, and because of this need for protection, more and more clans chose to join his ranks:

Ndwandwe and Mkwanazi, Koza and Nalovu, emaNewageni, Gumedi, Hlubi, Nguni, Bapedi. And from the heights of his new royal kraal he ruled his vast nation.

Powerful as the Matabele now were, however, peace was not to be. There were attacks by the Korana, by Dingaan (who had succeeded Shaka), the Basuto and the Griquas. The Basuto attack in particular had been devastating and Mzilikazi knew he would have to move again. Further west, this time. And so, in a seemingly never-ending column, weaving between the foothills, and swarming over the plains, the Matabele migrated once more. And when they reached the lush Marico district, they simply crushed the Bahurutsi who lived there – like an elephant crushes an anthill. Then they spread out, and started all over.

Mzilikazi built his famous eGabeni, with a high wooden palisade that protected his own royal kraal and harem. Military barracks were built at Mosega, with Mkalipi in charge of the regiments. He was protected on all sides. 'Here,' he thought, 'I will be safe. Here I will rest.'

And then, in August 1836, he received the terrible, shocking reports that people were coming over the rivers. His spies brought the news. 'They stream up like ants from the south. They come with their wagons and their cattle, their guns and their yellow servants. And they walk over the water of the rivers and now they camp in our territory.' He was stunned. They did not have permission. It was *his* country. What did they want? Their guns were dangerous. What should he do? What *could* he do?

Suddenly conscious of his *indunas* standing staring at him and jerked back to the present, Mzilikazi's great daydream came to an end. They had heard his story through, as they had done before, standing mutely before him, heads bowed. But at this point he needed advice, not a regiment of wooden statues. For the rest of the day they sat in parliament, and by the end of it, when the sun finally sank behind the olivewood trees, when the shadows fell thick on eGabeni and the sweat dried on their agitated faces, by the end of that day their minds were made up.

Mkalipi would leave the following morning. He would lead a regiment – one of the best – against the men who had crossed the Vaal.

'Barend! Barend! What is that noise?' Estella Liebenberg shook her husband awake. 'Listen! Do you hear it?' He turned to her; nodded. 'What is it, Barend? I have never heard such a noise before! It makes me shiver. Barend, *what is it?'*

Her husband climbed out of bed. Grabbing his muzzle loader in one hand, he thrust the flap of the tent aside and stepped out into the sharp, half-dark red-sky morning. A tall, gaunt man in a long white nightshirt.

The entire horizon was shaking and heaving. Coal-black figures, etched against the wakening sky, were creeping steadily forward. And as they advanced they rattled their shields and the dreadful hissing came nearer and nearer and still he stood limp, motionless, while they crept ever closer to the group of wagons, hunched up, sleeping, on the edge of the Vaal.

Inside the tent, Sara lay awake next to her mother. Too afraid to venture out, they lay together, trembling, heads turned to the open flap in the canvas. 'Papa has gone to see,' her mother told her. 'Everything will be alright, just lie very quietly.' But the terrible hissing came nearer, and Sara could lie there no longer. Flinging back the bedclothes, she burst from the tent and ran outside.

The Matabele were almost upon them, and a savage war-cry now rose from their ranks. A yell of triumph, a scream of rage. The earth moved as they stamped and beat out their war dance, pounding, shaking, rattling, closer and ever closer.

'Get back, Sara! Get back!' Her father, together with *Oom* Johannes and her *Oupa*, were loading their rifles. 'Get into the wagon at once!' But Sara could not move. She stood there, the early-morning breeze wrapping her nightdress around her legs, her long, fair hair blowing loose, her arms hanging limply at her sides.

Her eyes were wide with disbelief and horror and she could not move at all. She was not flesh and blood, her limbs were liquid, like hot candle wax.

Now she could see the monkey-tail kilts they wore round their hips, the circlets of ox tails above their elbows, the jackal skin capes. And on their heads those monstrous, leering feather headdresses. She could see their enormous, hairy shields and their assegaais and the screaming and stamping roared in her head and she could not move.

Sara heard the first deafening blast of musket fire. Then her legs buckled, and she fell to the ground.

When Sara opened her eyes, she saw that a man stood over her. The earth on which she lay was alive, it shook and pounded, the dust filled her nose and throat, her tongue stuck to her palate, she could not breathe. But worst of all was the smell. Sara did not know what it was, but the smell slapped against her in great bilious waves until she turned her head and threw up. It was the deathly stench of gunpowder, sweat and fear.

Still the man stood over her. Sara saw the shivering, sharp-pointed spear; above it the beaded black face; the nightmare of feathers and furs, the broad cracked feet with the ox tails twined above the ankles planted on either side of her head. She wanted her father. She had no voice, so she tried to get up, to find him. Like a striking snake the assegaai jabbed at her, forced her back onto the ground and kept her there.

When the man picked her up she did not struggle. It was all a dreadful dream, and her consciousness ebbed feebly and then lay still inside her. She knew she was being bumped and pushed and jostled and she didn't care. She simply slumped over his shoulder, and shut her eyes.

And then, like a sack of meal, but more gently, he off-loaded her onto a wagon. Sara felt the hard planks beneath her, and slowly she raised herself on one elbow and looked around. She recognised their old cedarwood kist, the big family Bible, the enamelled coffee pot with blue flowers. She was in *their* wagon and her parents were not there! The bed was terribly rumpled, and two chairs had been knocked over, and on the floor … on the floor … a thick, spreading, sliding red sheet of blood.

The wagon started to move. Not slowly, ponderously, with the comforting snort and jerk of the oxen she knew so well, but rapidly, almost wildly, wheels clanking over stones, and rocking from side to side. Sara got up to get away from the creeping, sticky blood that was now rolling to the front of the wagon. She looked out. The wheel of the wagon passed over the legs of a man. He was lying face downwards, his musket beside him, and

his back was soaked with blood and Sara screamed and screamed and when she eventually stopped, the screaming went on because Anna Maria and Christiaan had been thrust in with her, and they were screaming too.

Sara burst into tears at the sight of her brother and sister. Tears of relief, and tears of distress at their pale, terrified faces. She cried because Anna Maria was vomiting and because Christiaan's head was bleeding in a stream down the side of his neck; and they were being carted away in their family wagon. Not by the familiar span of black and white oxen, but by a bunch of black men with feathers on their heads and furs round their hips, all clutching the *disselboom* and trotting alongside: stamp – thud – stamp – thud, as their feet hit the ground. And behind them and beside them thundered the cattle, driven onwards by the force of the warriors behind.

For two full days and nights they travelled north in this manner, before Mkalipi demonstrated to Sara that she should show them how to make the oxen pull the wagon. She pointed out twelve strong oxen from the herd. The *riems* were there, the *disselboom* still intact. She was rewarded with several handfuls of berries and roots and a large calabash of curdled milk. The children were, by this time, weak from thirst and hunger and the food tasted very good to them. After this they were fed regularly, sometimes with strips of seared meat, always sour milk, occasionally some boiled pumpkin. Several times each day, when the oxen were changed, they were allowed to get off the wagon, but they were carefully watched and fetched if they wandered too far.

The plains stretched flat and endless. Waving grass, fertile valleys, scrubby trees, plenty of game. '*Konyana! Konyana!*' the men would call, pointing out prides of lions to the children. '*Konyana!* Grrr!' Once they came across piles of elephant droppings. A warrior drew an elephant in the sand with a stick. '*Enkholu*,' he told the children.

'*Enkholu*,' they repeated.

For fourteen long days they jolted northwards over the veld. A horde of triumphant warriors, three bewildered Voortrekker children, and the chief of the Matabele army, Mkalipi, who had spared their lives. Running beside the wagon, he told an uncomprehending Sara, 'We are going to take you to our king as a present! He will be pleased with you. And even more pleased with the cattle.'

He jabbered on, but Sara understood nothing. The only word she came to remember was eGabeni, through hearing it so often. And when they eventually reached the great kraal, and the name echoed and re-echoed throughout the ranks of soldiers, Sara realised that eGabeni was a place, and that they had arrived. She wanted to cry again. Physically, she had adjusted to sitting in the wagon, eating, sleeping, not thinking, just jolting over the veld. Now any change, anything new, flooded her with terror and a painful longing for her parents.

When they finally stopped, she retreated and lay under the bed, but Mkalipi soon found her. He lifted the children off the wagon, one by one, and hustled them through a large gap in a hedge of thorns. Inside, they saw little brown huts with low doors and

thatched roofs, between which they threaded a path, picking their way amongst stinking, rotten carcasses of wild animals, stepping over mounds of bleached bones, skins, and twisted horns. Through the opening in a high wooden fence they went, and suddenly all their escorts, everybody but Mkalipi, who walked beside them, fell down on their hands and knees and started crawling like dogs.

Before her, Sara saw a shortish, rather plump black man sitting on a stool. Round his waist, under his belly, he wore a leopard-tail kilt. On his head was bunched a plume of green feathers, and round his neck hung a necklace of brilliant, blue beads. He let out a loud exclamation of surprise when he saw the children. He pointed, the *indunas* jabbered, and when he spoke his voice was soft and quizzical, not harsh.

Christiaan began to cry, and Sara shushed him, realising they were being inspected and discussed. Then abruptly the conversation ceased. The man in front of them raised his arm and pointed to several large huts on his right, where his women stood in groups, peering, whispering together. Mkalipi urged the children on, calling to the women as he walked.

Two came forward. They were the largest women Sara had ever seen. With every step they took, their bellies wobbled and shook; ripples ran round their great arms and necks and their breasts billowed full and heavy, swinging from side to side. They took the children. Their bodies and ox-hide skirts smelt of animal fat, rank and stale, but they smiled timidly at the children, and held out their hands. And at this, the first real sign of affection in fourteen, harrowing days, they all three burst into tears and cried till their eyes swelled up and their breaths came in short, hiccupping gasps.

For two weeks the children stayed with the wives of the royal harem. They were well fed and cared for, and all day the women clucked round in astonishment and wonder, fingering their fair hair, gently touching their pale cheeks. The women taught them some words, pointing and repeating, then clapping their hands when the children repeated them after them. 'Mbali,' they said, pointing to the wild flowers in the veld. 'Mbali,' the children repeated. 'Isigodhlo,' they chanted, taking in the harem with a sweep of their wobbling arms. 'Induka,' they shouted, brandishing a *knobkierie* over a woolly head. 'Induka,' the children repeated. And the women repeated the children's names slowly. 'Sara, Anna Maria, Christiaan.' But they had difficulty with the R's and never mastered the pronunciation completely.

Most of the days were spent in and around the huts. Dome-shaped, the height of a tall man in the centre, criss-crossed with sticks and covered with several mats made from long grass, they were snug and watertight. To enter, the children had to bend double, while the adults crawled through on their bellies. Skirts and beads and the kilts of the men were piled onto platforms on one side, but there was no furniture and they slept flat on the hard ground, on mats of cypress.

At first the food made Sara nauseous, and she could only sit and watch as they ate, sometimes holding a whole sheep's stomach with its contents, bending over, tearing at it all together. At other times great wooden bowls of animal fat would be placed before them, together with boiled ribs, millet porridge, kidney beans and calabashes of sour milk. Hunger soon overcame Sara's aversion, and she ate. Stolidly, Anna Maria ate by her side. But Christiaan refused everything, and day by day he grew weaker and paler. Sometimes Sara would hold his head and force some thick milk between his lips. The women fussed around him and smeared dried blood on his stomach and the boiled juice of leaves on his forehead, but Christiaan would neither talk nor swallow. Eyes sunken, cheeks hollow, little legs shrivelled, he just lay. His heart was broken and he was alive only in that he still breathed.

Although they did not see him, Sara remained very afraid of the king, for she clearly remembered the words of her father. 'The Matabele are a powerful people,' he had said. 'We shall keep away from them for they are ruthless fighters and may not realise that we come in peace.'

So Sara remained very much in awe of Mzilikazi, but as she knew only kindness from the women, she could not remain afraid of them for long.

Her favourite was Mahlega, The One Who Laughs. She was the one who woke them in the mornings and took them down to the river to bathe with the other women and girls. Holding their hands tightly, Mahlega would splash and frolic with them in the cold, shallow pools. Unlike the older women, her body was still young and firm and Sara loved to watch her standing, quite naked, with the clear, sun-pricked drops sliding down her body. It was the colour of tobacco, a rich, burnished brown. The great wives of Mzilikazi took baths too, snorting and puffing, their flesh hanging loosely in soft folds, their beads glinting in the early morning sun. At first little Christiaan would also join them, but after a few days he was too weak and they had to leave him lying on his mat in the hut.

After bathing, Mahlega would rub their legs with a pink-tinted cream made from powdered clay, then she would help them wash their clothes, spreading them out on the bushes to dry. They had no linen *kappies* with them, no long print dresses, for they had been captured in their nightclothes, rather tattered now, drawn in at the neck and wrists with faded blue ribbon. And while these dried, they ran naked but for strings of beads which Mahlega hung round their necks. Each day their pale limbs grew browner, their stomachs filled out with maize and mabela, pumpkins and fatty meat. Yet they were often bewildered and unhappy, and Anna Maria cried a great deal.

'Never mind,' Sara would try to comfort her. 'Soon Papa will come galloping up on Pronk to fetch us and take all three of us back again to the wagons at the river.' Yet even as she spoke she knew, with childish instinct, that their Papa would never come. For the thing they had so often heard the men speak about, the thing the grown-ups had discussed only in lowered voices, when they thought the children were asleep, this thing had happened. The Matabele had come upon them and massacred their party.

During the day, Mahlega would take the girls to the fields with her. Here they sat in the shade of a tree and watched her hoeing the soil with the collar bone of an ox, in and out, over and over, until the midday sun burnt directly overhead. Then it was time to return to the harem, the *isigodhlo*, to clean the pots, cook some beans, perhaps, prepare a calabash of *amasi*, or weave new grass mats for them to sleep on.

In all this time they saw Mzilikazi only once. He sent for them one morning, when they returned from the river. Sara had to carry Christiaan, for he was too weak to walk. Mahlega went with them, dropping to her knees as they approached her lord and master. He wore the same blue beads round his neck, the same green feathers on his head; in his hand a calabash of beer, at his feet a bowl of red meat. At his side stood Mkalipi, the warrior who had captured Sara. She shrank when she saw him, for she remembered that face behind the assegaai, the huge feet planted on either side of her head. But Mahlega whispered soft, comforting words in her ear, and the king did not speak to them at all. Instead, he held a discussion with Mkalipi, speaking in his high-pitched voice, pointing from one child to the other.

'Soon I shall be visited by the white man, the hunter Captain Cornwallis Harris. It would be best if I get these white children out of the way before he comes. They are of his kind, and he will take them back.'

It wasn't that Mzilikazi was at all interested in the white children, but his favourite, Mkalipi, was. 'You want those little white lizards?' the king cried in astonishment. 'Those pale, thin sheep? You will be laughed at, Mkalipi! Come, let us cut off their heads and choose you two wives of whom you can be proud, who will bear you fine sons and and give you comfort and delight.' The *induna* shook his head. 'I will take other wives to bear me sons. But when these little sheep grow older, they will be able to teach me many things. They will share with me the knowledge of their fathers, and I shall be wise.' The king nodded thoughtfully and then, after several minutes, motioned to Mahlega to take them away.

One morning, soon after their summons by the king, Mahlega rushed into the hut, shook them awake and hustled them outside. There stood a young, pale-skinned man. 'Willem,' Mahlega said, pointing.

'Griqua.' Then she dashed inside and emerged with their rolled-up mats. To Sara's astonishment, the man Willem spoke to her in her own language. Broken and halting, but perfectly understandable. He had been part of a group of Griqua hunters who had slipped over the Orange. Most of them had been caught and killed by Mkalipi's warriors but, sensing that Willem might be useful in some way, his life had been spared. He was brought to live with the Matabele, and destined to become one of their headmen.

Now he told Sara that, on the instruction of the king, they were being sent to another kraal, to be looked after by Nyumbakazi, one of his wives who was childless. 'She has never had a child round her legs,' the king had said. 'She will be gentle with them and give them food and a mother's love.' Mahlega would accompany them. 'And Christiaan? We can't leave Christiaan!' Sara cried. 'He will follow later,' said Willem. 'The king will send him when he is stronger.'

Sara bit her lip and the tears rolled down her sunburned cheeks. She was unhappy and very afraid, she did not know where they were being taken, and the bushes were already cutting her feet.

It was an uneventful journey lasting seven days. Stolidly the little convoy made its way over the veld, sleeping by night beside a huge fire tended by Willem, to ward off any hungry leopards and lions.

By day they wove a path between the karee and mimosa trees, through the long spring green grass, keeping a sharp look-out for wild boars and buffaloes and hidden, deadly snakes. When their calabashes of *amasi* were empty, they drank at water holes, and Willem caught partridges and guinea fowl for them to eat, expertly breaking their necks like brittle sticks.

Stoically the little girls plodded on, their senses dulled through sheer exhaustion. To encourage them, Mahlega took out a surprise which she had kept hidden inside her sleeping mat: two small leather aprons, brightly decorated with beads. Pulling off their old, torn nightdresses, she slipped the little skirts, which she had spent many secret hours making, over their slender hips. Now they walked more confortably, and by the time they reached the kraal, their destination, their bodies were deeply browned and streaked with dust.

Nyumbakazi, their new mother, chuckled and fussed over them. Being childless, she was delighted to have two children to care for, and honoured by the king's decision to leave them in her care. If any harm befell them, her head would be cut off. So she cuddled them and fed them and chattered to them endlessly.

Quite soon, with both Nyumbakazi and Mahlega speaking to the children in their tribal tongue, they were fast learning to follow and even repeat certain short sentences. Sara found, too, that she was becoming used to sleeping on the ground; used to the taste of sour milk, greasy beans and thick millet porridge cooked in suet. But the sight of the paunch and fat of a beast, cooked together, unwashed, looking and smelling like dung, still made her stomach heave.

Soon, too, their bodies were burnt nut-brown and their fair hair was bleached white. It hung down their backs in two long ropes, tied by Mahlega with thin strips of soft leather. Their days were spent in gentle play and simple tasks, such as sweeping the floor of the hut with a reed broom, weaving sleeping mats and small baskets under Mahlega's guidance, helping to clear away the chaff on the threshing floor and then screaming with frightened delight when they flushed out mice from beneath the sheaves.

Gradually summer turned to autumn and the nights grew sharp and frosty. Sara and Anna Maria played at breathing out little white puffs of hot breath, seeing which one floated the furthest. 'I shall make you a kaross,' said Nyumbakazi. 'One for you, Sara, and one for the little one. See how it is done.'

First she put two leopard skins into the river overnight. Next day she washed them thoroughly, then laid them underneath the dung in the cattle kraal. When they were good and soft, she gave them a hard beating with a wooden mallet, another good wash, and then they were ready to use. The girls found them warm and comforting and seldom went without them. They spent much of their time now round the cosy fires, helping with the cooking, or just playing in sunny corners beside the walls of the huts, using bones and sticks as toys. They were well loved and well cared for, and slowly the painful, sharp edges of the past few months softened. The longing for their parents and the anguish of being lost and afraid was slowly, very slowly, receding.

Only the thought of Christiaan now tugged constantly at Sara's emotions. When she asked Mahlega about him, she just shook her head. Each day Sara spent a long while gazing at the scrubby horizon, hoping to see Willem appear with a small boy trotting by his side. But they never came. 'Perhaps they're waiting for the summer,' she told herself. 'After the rains.'

The rains came in October that year; strong, soaking rains that softened the earth in the fertile valley. And it was in the middle of the exciting, busy planting and tilling season that the Boers attacked.

It was very early one morning in November 1837. Sara was awake, staring heavy-eyed at the dying fire, seeking patterns in the embers, beasts in the spluttering, worn-out flames.

Then she sat up with a start. That was a shot! That was a gun! A thought flashed through her mind and left her breathless with the devastating impact – like a hard, physical blow. Perhaps her Papa had come to fetch her! He had found her, found them both at last! But just as quickly as it had surfaced, the thought died. Because she knew, had he been alive, he would have come long ago. She knew – had known all along – that he was killed that morning on the banks of the river. Killed by the thrust of an assegaai, like her mother and her baby brother. She had known this all along, but had pretended, twisting her daydreams, wringing them out of a bleak, dead knowledge. She did not even realise that she had accepted the brutal fact.

Now someone was firing a gun and Sara crawled to the opening of the hut and peered out. Outside all was confusion. Shouting and screaming, dazed, naked Matabele were pouring out of their huts. Some had had time to grab their assegais, others were simply running in terrified circles, trying to avoid the blasts of gunfire. On the ground men groaned and rolled in pain and the women screamed and, grabbing their children, fled into the bushes and forest on the hills above. Sara found herself being roughly wrapped in her kaross and flung across the back of a strong youth. Another grabbed Anna Maria. Like goats the men took off, up the hill, leaping from rock to rock, ducking and weaving until the children were eventually put down at the summit of a small hill.

Sara looked down. The scene was one of complete devastation. Once the commando had failed to find the small Boer children, they had set fire to the huts and granaries.

The air was thick with the acrid smell of gunpowder and smoke, and the village blazed like a mountain exploded.

Now the male warriors came scrambling up the hillside, fleeing before the bullets, against which their spears were useless. Frenziedly they herded the women and children together. 'Go!' they shouted. 'Go forward – to the north! We must flee!'

Sara took Anna Maria by the hand and followed, half-walking, half-running, not stopping to think that she was running away from her own people. Sara did not know that the Boer expedition was being led by Hendrik Potgieter, and that their chief aim was to find the Liebenberg children. She only knew that the smell of sweat and blood and gunpowder had triggered a half-buried memory; a slumbering, vicious nightmare. Screaming then, screaming and crying and calling, neither knowing nor caring, Sara ran away with the rest of the Matabele.

This routing was not the only humiliating defeat for the Matabele. There was Vegkop, when six thousand warriors surrounded a laager of just fifty Boer wagons. They crouched in the long grass all night, rattling their shields, slaughtering some oxen for food, rubbing their assegais in the blood. They knew that the Boers were watching them, knew that they must be very afraid. And then suddenly, as the sun rose, a handful of Boer men and boys rode out to meet them. A coloured man, acting as interpreter, addressed the Matabele. 'My master asks you,' he shouted, 'why you have come here today. Do you come to kill them? To steal their cattle? What harm have they done you that you should come upon them like this with your war cries and assegais and stabbing spears?' His words carried far on the clear morning air.

In answer, the Matabele regiments rose as one man. 'Mzilikazi!' they screamed, at the same time hurtling forward in a furious, pounding wave. With each step they took, they struck their knees on the insides of their shields, while with the other they stamped heavily on the ground, and the noise filled the skies like the ominous roll of thunder.

The Boers turned, and the wagons swallowed them up. The firing started, the guns tearing chasms in the enemy ranks, but still the Matabele came. When they reached the wagons they tried to pull them apart with their bare hands, but the wagons were chained together, the spaces between packed tightly with thorn bushes. It was a devastating battle but in the end Mkalipi signalled his warriors to leave, taking with them thousands of heads of cattle and sheep. These would offer some compensation when faced with their king's wrath.

The shining Matabele sun, it seemed, was on the wane. Vegkop, two attacks on Mosega, and a surprise attack by Dingaan which wiped out Mzilikazi's famous Guinea Fowl Regiment. His clever strategies were not working any longer. He knew instinctively that the next attack would be on eGabeni, his kraal, the last stronghold.

He worked out an extraordinary plan of action in which his warriors would hide behind a herd of cattle, and then goad them into stampeding right over the enemy, tearing them apart with their hooves and their horns. The plan could not fail. It did. And so the Matabele fled. Early in 1838, disheartened and beaten, the entire nation migrated northwards, moving slowly in the direction of the great Limpopo River.

They split into two streams – the old men, women and children went ahead, led by Gudwani Ndwini. They were followed by the king, leading his unhappy army with Maggekeni Sithole as the leading *induna*. Holding Anna Maria by the hand, Sara slipped and stumbled over the sharp rocks on the mountain. She did not fully comprehend the reason behind the flight, but Mahlega and Nyumbakazi were going, and that was reason enough for her to follow. The motherly black women were the only symbols of security in her troubled world, and she now trotted obediently along with the other children.

Day after day, week after week, the march continued. Although they had started off at the height of the rainy season, often trudging through ankle-deep mud and pouring rain, having to be carried across swollen rivers on the backs of the warriors and sleeping at night on mounds of sodden grass, now there was no rain. There was nothing but the burning sun beating down relentlessly on the stream of refugees crossing the bushveld.

One scorching day followed another. As a nation, they were terrified of the dark; travelling in the cool of the evening was unthinkable. When the sun set they would lie down to sleep behind rocks, or in flimsy shelters, made of poles and swathes of grass. And when the first rays of the sun flooded the veld, when the earth began to bake and crackle after the brief respite of the night, they would rise and set off again.

Their calabashes of meal had long since been emptied; their cattle were thin and there was little milk; they subsisted mainly on roots and berries, sucking out the juices to ease their thirst.

Slowly the column moved north-east towards the Zout-pansberg mountains. They marched in silence, shuffling without energy or spirit, fatigued and ill. Then the old people and the children started dying. Sometimes they simply fell back and lay down, too weak even to seek the shade of a camelthorn bush. Sometimes they simply did not get up in the morning. And if the others protested at leaving them behind, one of the warriors – the Amnyama Makanda – would move in and club them to death.

Sara, now very weak and thin, floundered on. Her oxhide skirt was torn and filthy, her bright beads long since broken and lost, her entire body covered in thick dust. Flies crawled round her nose and mouth and listlessly she fanned them away. Anna Maria was dying and she knew it. She had never been as sturdy as Sara and once dysentery struck, she had no reserves. Her face grew pinched and her fever rose. Her ribs protruded and the water poured down her legs. They had long ago lost Mahlega. Then late one afternoon Anna Maria fell down, and did not respond to Sara's pleas to try and rise. Nyumbakazi squatted down beside her and waved Sara on. When Sara refused to move, a young soldier came up and Nyumbakazi spoke to him rapidly. Lifting his club high over his head, he lunged forward on one leg and brought the club down onto a bush. The dry branches split and spat their dead foliage onto the ground. 'Forward!' he commanded Sara. 'Forward!' And he brought the club down again, this time nearer to where she was standing.

Lightheaded from hunger and fatigue, Sara moved forward obediently. She moved forward, trance-like, with the children who were still able to walk. Anna Maria's death was the final blow to her bruised consciousness. Perhaps this ultimate severing with her past made it easier for her to accept the present. Now she was no-one. So she picked up the children who had fallen. She treated their cut feet with juice squeezed from leaves.

She spoke to them in their own language, for by now she understood much and could communicate with ease.

One evening, at the end of an arduous day threading their way between the rocks and crags of the Zoutpansberg mountains, Sara found a young woman collapsed at the side of the track. Perspiration was streaming down her face, her body was shaking with fever, and she was babbling deliriously. On her lap lay a tiny naked infant; by her side sat a small boy, his face covered with scabs, his stomach grossly enlarged, snivelling.

Two women stopped. 'It is Fulata, the king's wife,' said one. 'The Swazi woman.'

'Then we must help her,' replied the other.

'No, no. If she dies, or her children die, the king will blame us. Let us rather pretend we never saw her. We shall know nothing about it. The vultures will do the rest.'

And they wandered on.

Sara had half a calabash of sour milk. She was one of the lucky few who had slept near several cows the previous night, and managed to squeeze a small quantity of milk from the shrivelled udders in the morning. Now she dropped some, little by little, into the baby's mouth and then passed the calabash to the boy who lifted it and swallowed greedily. 'Nyumbakazi!' she called 'Nyumbakazi, come! They will die if we do not help them! It is growing dark and their mother is very sick and the wild beasts will come and eat them! We must help them, Nyumbakazi!'

'Yes, it is Fulata,' said gentle Nyumbakazi, bending down. 'And the look of death is already in her eyes.' Carefully the old woman laid her down on the yellow grass. 'She will not see the sun rise in the morning. But we will take the children. They are Ningi and Lobengula and my master will not be pleased if I leave his children here to be eaten by the lions and picked at by the vultures.'

So saying, she picked up the baby, Ningi, and told Sara to take the boy's hand. 'Carry him, if you can, when he gets tired,' she told her.

Gently, Sara picked up her frail little charge and together she and the small boy descended the mountain. Lobengula – 'He Who Drives Like The Wind' – and his strange, new foster mother.

For Lobengula, Sara searched out the juiciest berries; scooped the mountain water over his face when they came across a stream; saved for him any *amasi* she could beg or steal.

By day she picked bunches of grass to help Nyumbakazi shield the infant Ningi from the sun, and by night she collected bunches of soft, evergreen leaves for their beds.

Unexpectedly, they found themselves in the old country of the Crocodile People where a few settlements still flourished. Spurred by their hunger, they ransacked the granaries stacked with grain, ripped bare the fields of melon, pumpkins and corn and then, with renewed strength they crossed the treacherous, mosquito-infested swamps that lay in their path and found themselves on the northern banks of the Limpopo River. Now the women danced and clapped with joy for here the grass waved as high as a man's shoulder; here antelope abounded; there were bubbling streams and clear blue skies and tall, flowering trees.

A rumour spread that Gudwane would soon call a halt. This was good, fertile country and their king would surely catch up with them soon, leaving the threat of armed Boers and the menace of Dingaan far behind. And so, thankfully, they built a village on the plains. At last the weary tribe was able to settle down and start planting their crops.

Sara and her small charge, now a fat, strong little boy, became a familiar sight in the village. Still too young to be sent out herding calves, Lobengula was able to spend all his time with his foster mother.

Sara was growing tall. Her face and body – now deeply browned – and her bright blue eyes, contrasted strangely with the rich colour of her skin. Her hair was still very long and fair, but she was no longer so thin and wiry. She was filling out slowly, her legs were sturdier, her hips slightly rounded, and, because she was so gentle and kind, the others called her Little Mother. But although she cared for and played with any child who crossed her path, Lobengula was her chief concern, her only interest. For all the love she would normally have given to her mother and father, her sister and brother, she now lavished on him. He was her child; her plaything; the substitute for her family; and her solid little anchor in a tumultuous world.

When Sara went with the other young girls to hoe the fields, Lobengula went with her. 'Come and sit with me,' she would sometimes call. 'Come and sit with me under the Moshokaphala tree and let us catch its tears.' Little drops fell from the clusters of purple flowers on the Moshokaphala tree – fine sprinklings of drops, sliding from the beautiful coloured trusses. 'Look, the tree is raining,' Sara would say, and Lobengula would rush, laughing, trying to catch the drops as they fell. At other times she would fashion a span of oxen from the river mud. 'They are yours, for you are a rich king. Here are your huts,' and she would pile little stones one on top of the other, 'and here are your people,' scratching open a nest of ants. 'See how they hurry backwards and forwards. They are building for their king, and finding food. Do not stamp on them, or they will rise and bite you.' And she would pinch his arm and, laughing, run away as he tried to catch her.

Sara taught her foster child not to touch the scorpions under the stones, and to retreat from snakes and spiders. She taught him which fruits were good to eat and which would make him sick. And at night, when they sat round the fires, and the old women told tales of magic and the spirits of ancestors, Sara whispered little stories of her own to Lobengula. And he would sit enchanted, enormous black eyes never leaving her face, as she told of guns and horses and white rolling wagons; of chairs and tables and quill pens and bonnets.

'Come, Sara,' the women would sometimes call after the evening meal. 'Let us dance now! Leave your little black rabbit and let us sing and stamp and clap our hands!' And Sara would get up and join the women, first putting Lobengula, heavy as he now was, on her back, where she tied him securely inside a skin. She was learning to sway and to chant; most of the songs of the Matabele were repetitive, went on and on, with little tune to them and no more than six words, so they were easy to learn. And Lobengula would fall asleep on her back, and wake up in the morning to find that she had gently put him to sleep on the mat beside hers, and was already up and sweeping the floor.

'She works like an old Matabele woman,' the others laughed, pointing at her. 'Our little white bird, you work too hard!' Sara would smile and continue her job grinding dry tobacco leaves with which to make snuff. Nyumbakazi enjoyed taking snuff, and kept it packed tightly into small horns which she hung round her neck, or stuck into her ear hole.

After twelve months had passed, the village – with its domed huts nestling inside a high hedge – was flourishing. The rains had come in time, and they were able to harvest good crops of pumpkins and corn and maize. The cattle were fat, and game was plentiful. They were hungry no longer.

'Au! Look how she runs, my young white antelope, my little *magogo*,' Nyumbakazi said one day, as she and several other women sat weaving beer strainers from the strong grass that grew so abundantly. 'Her legs are as long as a giraffe's.'

'Yes, she will soon be a woman, Nyumbakazi,' another answered. 'It is time she set aside her small apron now, and you must give her a proper girl's cloth to her knees.' Nyumbakazi nodded. 'She is tall like a woman but she has not the body of our young girls. See how flat are her nipples, still, and how slender her buttocks. She is like a reed by the river, and although I love her greatly, though my heart is as white as milk when I think of her, yet I do not believe she is a desirable young girl. She will not be looked at by any of *our* men. A woman must be soft; her breasts full and ripe; her thighs large and warm.'

'Au! Do you not remember how thin the man Moffat was also?' the other asked. 'Perhaps it is the way of the white people.'

So they dressed Sara in a longer skin apron and hung more beads around her neck and wrists and bracelets round her ankles, but Sara only found these ornaments a nuisance, and she and Lobengula took them off and played with them in the sand. They played in the sand, and worked in the fields, and bathed in the river – two children, one orphaned, one motherless, who grew closer and more dependent on each other every day, little dreaming that Mzilikazi was about to return and that soon their world would, once more, be shattered.

The Great Bull Elephant was not dead, as so many had come to believe. He and his army had been put to flight by their old enemies, the Makololo, and had fled south-wards, finally coming to rest at the Mahrikari Salt Pans, south-east of the Okavango. Little did they know that they were only ten marching days away from the rest of the clan. Nor did Mzilikazi know that there was talk of choosing another king.

The truth of the matter was that there was a lack of law and order in the kraal. Old uMncumbata, the regent, was inefficient and had been banished.

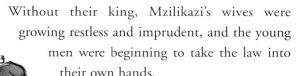

Without their king, Mzilikazi's wives were growing restless and imprudent, and the young men were beginning to take the law into their own hands.

'Let us crown Kulumane! He is the king's eldest son and the rightful heir to the throne. And because he is still young, we will put a regent in his place for a while.'

'Never!' retorted the other *indunas*. 'We say our king is still alive! And we shall search for him, the length and breadth of the country, before we will accept a new king.'

They found Mzilikazi at the Salt Pans. 'So they planned to put Kulumane on the throne, did they? The dogs! The sons of foxes! They would make my son, that yellow lizard, the king – while I, The Great King, am still alive? Lead me to the people at once! You say certain *indunas* wanted to put Kulumane on the throne? Then they shall die!' He screwed up his eyes, banging his fist. 'I will kill them all! And my son shall be first. You will twist his neck. Snap! Like a chicken. And call the people to come and see that their king, The Great Bull Elephant, is alive!'

The following day Mzilikazi issued another command which would ensure that he was, once again, the undisputed king of the tribe.

'You have done away with Kulumane,' he said. 'Now you must take the other sons too. Ubuhlelo. And Lobengula.' With all three members of his family directly in line to the throne put out of the way, he would be safe. So Ubuhlelo was put to death. 'But where was Lobengula?' the *indunas* whispered amongst themselves. 'We saw him only a short while ago.' Enquiries revealed nothing. The women shook their heads. 'We do not know where he is. He and his white mother have gone.'

And where were Sara and Lobengula?

Life in the kraal had become more and more unpleasant for the two children. Umoaka, mother of Kulumane, was a cruel and jealous woman. In Lobengula, she had, for a long time, seen a future threat to her son, and she mulled over ways of getting rid of them. 'Scum of the earth!' she would mutter, her enormous body shaking with anger. 'Toads! Wretched, yellow spawn of frogs!' And she would spit at them. 'The crocodiles will have you! For I, I alone, am the king's great wife and only *my* children are royal. Kulumane will be king! A great Black Calf! Eater of the Sun! But you, Lobengula – you and your sick-white playmate – you shall know nothing of it for you will be lying at the bottom of the river!'

Umoaka did not know that by driving them away, she was actually saving Lobengula from being killed by his father. Her wrath had frightened Sara so much that she had lain awake all night making plans. Pictures of hundreds of men and women who had, for various reasons, been put to death, now flashed before her eyes. The writhing figures with sharp poles stuck up through their bodies, left to the vultures who swooped in before they were dead; the screaming women who, bound with thongs, were tossed into the river like bundles of chaff; others, with lips or ears or hands sliced off. All night she lay and schemed, and very early in the morning, when the blackness of the night turned to grey and the stars paled, and the cattle started their clumping and blowing, she slid out from under her *kaross* and prepared to leave.

Taking a large wooden pail, she filled it with corn, a hunk of goat's meat and stewed beans. Then she woke Lobengula, putting her finger to his lips, wrapping his *kaross* round his shoulders. Crossing to where Nyumbakazi lay, fast asleep, Sara bent down and kissed the wrinkled forehead. How kind she had been to them! 'Dear Nyumbakazi, do not think badly of me,' she whispered. 'It must be done; we have to go now.'

Together they walked past the sleeping huts and into the bush.

The sky was turning from flame to gold, the birds singing shrilly in their hidden nests, the earth already beginning to throb with the approach of another hot day, when they found themselves on the top of a rise overlooking a valley. The valley was spiked with mopani trees and sharp cactuses and ringed by a tumble of granite boulders which rose steadily higher to the peak beyond. Here, high above the valley towered M'lindidzimo – the mountain of Ngwali, the ancient high priest of the Makalanga.

On the morning that Sara and Lobengula rested under the mopani tree, Ngwali was sitting high above, watching them. His shrewd little eyes missed nothing. He had seen them the instant they emerged from the forest and by the time they lay down under a mopani tree next to the stream to sleep, his plans were already made.

Ngwali chuckled to himself. Was fortune not playing right into his hands? His ancestors knew that he was eternally resentful of the Matabele invaders; that he was always watchful for ways in which he might rid his country of this conquering tribe – they who had butchered his people and feasted on their corn. Perhaps his chance for revenge lay right down there, in the valley, fast asleep!

He would, of course, send his women to go and fetch them. Once in his possession, he could put them to good use. Very good use indeed! Ngwali sat outside his cave, thoughtfully drawing pictures in the sand with a mopani twig. Down in the south, near the Zoutpansberg, lived the white people, the Boers. He knew of their leader, the man

called Potgieter or Enteleka; and he had heard from his spies that Enteleka still sought the white children. 'I shall send word to him,' he muttered. 'I shall send messages with the Bechuana hunters. They shall tell him that a white girl is being held at the kraal. That she is being treated badly.' Then, without a doubt, the Boers would come thundering up from the south. There would be a clash, perhaps even a war. 'And if the power of the Matabele is broken? Au! The country will at last be returned to my people – the Makalanga!'

Ngwali opened his little leather pouch and threw the contents on the ground before him: the ankle joint of a monkey, the eye of a crocodile, the bladder of a lion, a few shrivelled seedpods and a dead night adder. His beady eyes shone. The signs were good, *very* good indeed.

When Sara and Lobengula woke, the sun was already sinking in the west. Sara sat up, rubbing her eyes, not knowing where she was, not knowing who these women were who sat watching her. They spoke, and although the language was strange, there were some words that Sara did understand.

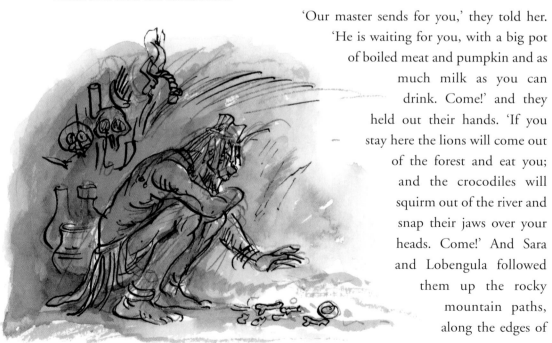

'Our master sends for you,' they told her. 'He is waiting for you, with a big pot of boiled meat and pumpkin and as much milk as you can drink. Come!' and they held out their hands. 'If you stay here the lions will come out of the forest and eat you; and the crocodiles will squirm out of the river and snap their jaws over your heads. Come!' And Sara and Lobengula followed them up the rocky mountain paths, along the edges of precipices, squeezing through gaps between giant boulders, climbing up and up until, when it was very late and very dark, they came to a village, and to Ngwali – head of the mountain priests and wizards.

Now Sara felt more at ease. She could not imagine why Ngwali had sent for them, but it was good to be among such friendly people and safe from the wild animals that prowled at night. The two young refugees settled very happily into their new life on the mountain. They were kindly treated and well fed and the eerie fabric of witchcraft and sorcery held endless fascination for them and occupied much of their time.

Only one member of the Matabele tribe knew of their whereabouts. This was uMncumbata, the old regent who had been driven out because he had been unable to control the *indunas* and the royal wives during the king's absence. Now he lived on the fringes of the settlement, and had befriended the priests on the mountain, who threw bones for him, and gave advice in return for a sheep or a beast.

uMncumbata often visited the children , and he kept their secret. 'You are safest here,' he reasoned. 'They searched for you for many days in the village, and Nyumbakazi wept and wailed for a long time. But no-one was brave enough to tell the king. Mzilikazi thinks that you are dead, Lobengula, and therefore no longer a threat to him.' The children now felt truly secure and happy in their mountain hide-out with the Makalanga women, under the protection of Ngwali.

They remained inseparable, this young boy and his devoted guardian. Sara felt responsible for him, like a mother feels responsible for the welfare of her child, and to Lobengula her presence meant security and constant attention. Instead of learning to herd his father's cattle, join the military and become a blood-thirsty warrior, Lobengula grew up with witchcraft on one hand and the gentleness of the Dutch girl on the other.

And then one morning in the year 1847, while Lobengula was teaching Sara how to skin a buck, while they stood at the top of their mountain with the bloody skin spread-eagled across a rock at their feet, they saw, far below, a stream of men on horseback. Ngwali had sent his message. Enteleka had come.

'Look, Sara! What are those?' Lobengula shouted excitedly. 'Great buck carrying their young on their backs?' Sara straightened up and looked. Suddenly her heart was pounding in her head, the blood rushed from her face and there was a terrible drumming in her ears.

She swayed and sat down as a host of distant memories burst painfully upon her. People, scenes, events she had thought were dreams, unreal and half-forgotten, now appeared sharply etched in her mind. Those men, she knew, with a sudden, terrible knowledge, were her people. And they had come to fetch her.

'Sara, what *are* they?' Lobengula repeated once more.

'They are white people,' she answered faintly. '*My* people.'

'White people?' he asked incredulously. uMncumbata had once told him stories about the white people and of how they had fought the Matabele with sticks that spat out stones that killed, and of how assegais were useless against these sticks. These people, uMncumbata had said, were to be greatly feared. *Never* had he imagined that Sara could be one of them! White was white, and she was brown as the earth. Her hair was different, of course, and her eyes, but she was no more white than a brown heifer was white. He was confused and puzzled. 'I must tell uMncumbata,' he decided, and hurried down the rocky path that led to uMncumbata's small settlement.

'No! Lobengula, wait! Wait! You must not ... Wait!' But her words were lost on the wind. There was nothing she could do but follow him. She met them halfway down the path. uMncumbata had been on his way up, when Lobengula had nearly knocked him over. Now they sat in the shade of a rock and talked excitedly.

'The time has come,' the old man was saying, patting the ground beside him for Sara to sit down. 'The time has come for me to take you, Lobengula, back to your father.

As you know, he thinks you are dead – so he might be very angry – but I think,' and the old man drummed his fingers on the boy's knee, 'I think if you were to warn him about these people you have seen coming into our country, I think if you were to tell him that they might surprise him, he will be ready in case of an attack. Then he might be very pleased with you, and keep you in the royal kraal. Then you will be the next king and you will be good to your old friend uMncumbata.'

Lobengula jumped up. 'Show me the way to my father! Quickly! If what you say is true, then I must go to tell him!'

'Lobengula!' Sara called. 'Wait! Stay! Don't leave me here!'

But he was already running down the path. 'I'll come back, Sara!' he called over his shoulder. 'It could be dangerous for you to come with me. Go now, and wait for me on the mountain.'

Slowly Sara turned and walked back, her mind in turmoil. Who *was* she? And where lay her destiny? Would she always belong to a great booming bearded man, who had picked her up and hugged her and given her toys and told her stories? Or did she belong to Nyumbakazi, who had fed and cared for her when she was lost and afraid? Or to Ngwali, who had sheltered her so kindly? Or to Lobengula – first her child – and then her companion and brother? But *her* father's people and *his* father's people were enemies,

and he was Mzilikazi's son, the prince of the tribe – and the future king. And so who was she – and where could she go?

When Sara reached her hut she entered through the small low door and blinked in the gloom inside. She felt for her calabash. It was full. Then she selected a small basket, filled it with millet meal, wrapped it carefully in a leather pouch and tucked it into her rolled-up *kaross*. Holding her possessions tightly, Sara crept through the doorway, stepped out onto the sunlit path, and walked into the forest.

In March 1870, Lobengula was installed as king of the Matabele.

Lily reached for her handkerchief up her sleeve, wiped her forehead and settled back, hands folded. No-one said a word, they all just sat and looked at her. Eventually Victoria broke the silence. 'Is that a true story, Lily?'

Lily shrugged. 'Perhaps, perhaps not. Nobody knows, and nobody ever will. It's word-of-mouth. History.'

'*Sjoe!* Now I need a coffee,' said Sophia.

They nodded, pulled on their jerseys, folded their notebooks and put away their pencils. And with Victoria leading the way they walked down the street, straight past The Coffee Shop, and into the ladies' bar at the Corriebush Arms.

Bibliography

Not much has been much written about Sara and, due to some conflicting facts and opinions, a story such as this could only be woven and cobbled together by the author with the help of exploratory reading, the use of relevant research books – and personal imagination. Grateful acknowledgement goes to the following.

Becker, P. *Path of Blood*. Longman's Green & Co Ltd, 1962.

Brett, BLW. *Makers of South Africa*. T Nelson & Sons Ltd, 1944.

Bulpin, TV. *The Great Trek*. Books of Africa, Cape Town, 1969.

Cloete, S. *African Portraits*. Constantia Publishers, Cape Town, 1969.

Cowley, C. *Kwazulu*. C Struik (Pty) Ltd, Cape Town, 1966.

De Klerk, W. *The Puritans in Africa*. Rex Collings, London, 1975.

De Villiers, A. *Stage Coach Adventures and other South African Tales*. Afrikaanse Pers Boekhandel.

Fisher, J. *Die Afrikaners*.

Hole, HM. *The Passing of the Black Kings*. Rhodesiana Reprint Library and in particular his book, *Lobengula*. P Allan & Co Ltd, London, 1929.

Howcroft, P. *South African Encyclopaedia: Prehistory to the year 2000*. Unpublished papers with SA History Online. [http://www.sahistory.org.za/pages/people/mzilikazi.htm].

Meintjies, J. *The Voortrekkers*. Cassell & Co Ltd, London, 1973.

Moffat, R. *Matabele Journals*. Chatto & Windus, London, 1945.

'Mziki: Mlimo*. Natal Witness, Pietermaritzburg, 1926.

Nathan, M. *The Voortrekkers of South Africa*. Central News Agency Ltd, South Africa/ Gordon & Gotch Ltd, London, 1937.

Omer-Cooper, JD. *The Zulu Aftermath*. Longman's Green & Co Ltd, 1966.

Preller, G. *Lobengula*. Afrkaanse Pers Boekhandel, Johannesburg, 1963.

Ransford, O. *The Great Trek*. J Murray (Pty) Ltd, London, 1972.

Raper, PE. *New Dictionary of South African Place Names*. Jonathan Ball Publishers (Pty) Ltd, Johannesburg & Cape Town, 2004.

Roberts, B. *The Zulu Kings*. Hamish Hamilton Ltd, 1974.

The Diary of Erasmus Smit: Minister to the Voortrekkers (HF Schoon) translated by WGA Mears. C Struik (Pty) Ltd, Cape Town, 1972.

Summers, R & Pagden, CW. *The Warriors*. Books of Africa, Cape Town, 1970.

Theal, GM. *History of the Boers in South Africa*. Struik (Pty) Ltd, Cape Town, 1973.

Walker, EA. *The Great Trek*. A&C Black, London, 1938.

Desserts

Cinnamon Poached Pears with Nut Liqueur

A memorable dessert, this one, supremely elegant and yet so easy to prepare – plus there are options: you can use either Amaretto and almonds, or Frangelico and hazelnuts; you can serve the pears plain to relish the fine flavours; with crème fraîche to offset the sweetness; or with a blob of mascarpone piled into the hollows. Very special, any which way.

4 large pears (700–800 g),
unblemished and not quite ripe
fresh lemon juice
500 ml (2 cups) water
125 ml (½ cup) sugar
2 fat sticks cinnamon
45–60 ml (3–4 Tbsp) Amaretto OR
Frangelico liqueur
toasted almonds OR roasted
hazelnuts*, coarsely crushed

Peel the pears as smoothly as possible, halve, and nick out the pips and core. Brush the rounded sides with lemon juice. Bring the water, sugar and cinnamon to the boil in a wide-based frying pan. Add the pears, rounded sides up, in a single layer. Cover and simmer gently for about 30 minutes. Test with the tip of a skewer – they should be soft but definitely not mushy. Using a slotted spoon, remove the pears from the poaching liquid and arrange them in a shallow dish to fit snugly, rounded sides up. Discard the cinnamon. Turn up the heat and boil the poaching liquid rapidly, uncovered, for 10–12 minutes, or until very bubbly, a pale toffee colour, and reduced to about 150 ml (⅔ cup). Remove from the stove, stir in the chosen liqueur, and slowly pour the syrup over the pears. Leave to cool, basting a few times, then cover and refrigerate for a few hours. Sprinkle with the nuts before serving. **Serves 4–8.**

* If using hazelnuts, remove the loose skins after roasting by rubbing the nuts in a clean kitchen towel.

Fruit Flops

These are top favourites on the dessert menu and even those who shy away from rich mousses always flip for flops – tropical fruit under a blanket of cream, yoghurt and a tipple of alcohol. Another plus is that they need to be assembled hours in advance, and then just left to do their thing in the refrigerator until dinner time. Important points: use a bowl or goblets that are wide at the top; the cream mixture should be thick, but still pourable; and in order to soften and melt, the sugar must be sprinkled on thinly and evenly.

Very Simple Flop

2–3 large, firm but ripe bananas, peeled and cut into small dice

fresh lemon juice

2–3 large, firm but ripe mangoes, peeled and cut into small pieces (400 g prepared weight)

125 ml fresh cream

a few drops of vanilla essence OR extract

60 ml (4 Tbsp) thick, low-fat plain Bulgarian yoghurt

15 ml (1 Tbsp) dark rum

40 ml (8 tsp) soft brown sugar

Toss the bananas in a little lemon juice, mix with the mango flesh, then spoon into four glass bowls or wide goblets, dividing equally. (Glass is preferable to pottery, so that you can see the layers.) Whip the cream with the vanilla, then fold in the yoghurt and rum. Pour over each serving of fruit, and sprinkle each with 10 ml (2 tsp) soft brown sugar (use your fingers.) Refrigerate for 4–6 hours, or until the sugar just starts to melt. **Serves 4 and is easily doubled.**

Elegant Flop

3 large, firm but ripe mangoes, peeled and cubed (500 g prepared weight)

1 x 565 g can pitted litchis, drained, patted dry and slivered

1 large knob preserved ginger, finely chopped

1 x 175 ml tub thick, plain Bulgarian yoghurt

30–45 ml (2–3 Tbsp) Amaretto liqueur

a few drops of vanilla essence OR extract

200 ml (⅘ cup) fresh cream, whipped

45 ml (3 Tbsp) soft brown sugar

toasted almond flakes to decorate

Mix the prepared fruits and ginger and spoon into one glass bowl or divide between six small bowls or goblets. Fold the yoghurt, Amaretto and vanilla into the whipped cream. Pour over the fruit to cover completely. Using your fingers, sprinkle the sugar over evenly. Refrigerate for 4–6 hours, or until the sugar starts to melt. Sprinkle with almonds before serving. **Serves 6.**

Cheesecake Pots

These are light, novel and, dressed as they are in red and magenta, they make you feel cheerful even before you dip in your spoon. Similar to cheesecake, but without any crust to interfere with the delicate flavour, and no egg yolks. Remember that the cottage/cream cheese must be at room temperature (or else the gelatine could make strings when added) and the egg whites at room temperature as well, or they won't whip. Another point: when a recipe requires vanilla, use either essence or extract. The latter is excellent, but far more expensive, and many cooks do not have it in their store cupboards, but if you do, use less than essence.

Strawberry Pots

250 g strawberries, rinsed and hulled
90 ml (6 Tbsp) castor sugar
1 x 250 g tub smooth, low-fat cottage cheese
12 ml (2½ tsp) gelatine
60 ml (¼ cup) water
125 ml (½ cup) fresh cream
a few drops of vanilla essence
2 XL free-range egg whites
extra strawberries to decorate
strawberry coulis and extra cream

STRAWBERRY COULIS

Blend 250 g strawberries with 30 ml (2 Tbsp) castor sugar until smoothly puréd. To spark the flavour you could add a tipple of orange liqueur, but this is optional. Makes about 350 ml (1⅖ cups).

Slice the strawberries and place in a processor fitted with the metal blade. Add half the sugar and leave to stand for 10 minutes to draw the juices. Add the cottage cheese and pulse just until smoothly combined. Don't puré to a mush – the mixture should be pale pink and flecked with little bits of berries. Turn into a large bowl. Sponge the gelatine in the water, dissolve over simmering water, and slowly stir into the cheese mixture. Whip the cream with the vanilla, and fold in. Whisk the egg whites until fairly stiff, then slowly add the remaining 45 ml (3 Tbsp) sugar to make a glossy meringue mixture. Stir a spoon of this through the strawberry mixture, then fold in the remainder gently but thoroughly. Pour into eight rinsed ramekins (about 6 cm diameter, 5 cm deep) or moulds and refrigerate until set. Unmould onto individual serving plates. Decorate each with one fresh berry, pour the coulis around each little pud, and run a ribbon of the extra cream through the bright coulis. **Serves 8.**

Cherry Amaretto Pots

Pot and unmould, or use wide-brimmed glasses or bowls – either way it looks beautiful.

2 x 250 g smooth, low-fat
cottage cheese
125 ml (½ cup) castor sugar
a small pinch of salt
75–90 ml (5–6 Tbsp) Amaretto liqueur
a few drops of vanilla essence
20 ml (4 tsp) gelatine
60 ml (¼ cup) water
250 ml (1 cup) fresh cream, whipped
3 XL free-range egg whites
extra 60 ml (4 Tbsp) castor sugar

TOPPING
1 x 425 g can stoned black cherries,
drained (reserve syrup)
2 ml (½ tsp) cornflour
60 ml (¼ cup) reserved cherry syrup
whipped cream to decorate

Whisk together the cottage cheese, sugar, salt, liqueur and vanilla until smooth. Sponge the gelatine in the water and dissolve over simmering water, then slowly drizzle into the cheese mixture, whisking rapidly. Fold in the whipped cream. Whisk the egg whites until peaking, then gradually add the extra castor sugar while whisking to a stiff meringue. (If you do this first, and work quickly, you won't have to wash the beaters.) Stir a spoonful of the meringue into the creamy cheese mixture, then fold in the remainder. Pour or spoon levelly into 8–10 ramekins (about 6 cm diameter, 5 cm deep) or glasses and refrigerate until set. To prepare the topping, dry the cherries with paper towels, then carefully halve them, using a sharp knife. Unmould the cheesecake pots, or leave in the serving bowls. Arrange cherries, rounded sides up, on top of each dessert. Slake the cornflour with the reserved cherry syrup, then boil for a few minutes until thick, while stirring. Cool briefly, then use to glaze the cherries, using a pastry brush. Pipe rosettes of cream in the open spaces and refrigerate until serving time. **Serves 8–10.**

Frankly Fruity

Serving fresh fruit with cheese (instead of a dessert) is in good taste and becoming increasingly popular, because it's so much better for everyone. One step further is to serve Fruidites (a selection of sliced fresh fruit) with a creamy dip such as gingered mascarpone; the third option is to start off with fresh fruit and then doll it up. The following desserts fall into this category, and they are both best served with a top-quality vanilla ice cream, rather than crème fraîche or whipped cream. And – good news – they need to be made at least 24 hours in advance and refrigerated, so that the flavours can marry and mellow.

Minted Watermelon With Gin

ripe watermelon
250 ml (1 cup) water
30 ml (2 Tbsp) sugar
about 15 fresh, new mint leaves (not big old ones)
gin
extra fresh mint

This is for 4 large or 6 small servings. Use a melon baller to scoop the watermelon flesh into little globes, discarding the pips. Divide between glass dessert bowls or wide goblets, allowing 200–250 ml (⅘–1 cup) balls per serving. Bring the water and sugar to the boil in a small saucepan, stirring at first to dissolve the sugar. Boil rapidly for 4–5 minutes. The mixture will be very bubbly but only slightly reduced, as it's a really light syrup – watermelons are so sweet that a heavy syrup would be quite wrong. Cool the syrup, then add the mint leaves and mix very briefly in a blender – don't blend well, you want to see the flecks of mint. Spoon 7 ml (1½ tsp) gin over each serving – this may seem very little, but it just adds something special to the flavour. Then spoon 30–45 ml (2–3 Tbsp) syrup over each – the syrup will be enough for 4 large or 6 smaller servings. Finally snip 1 extra mint leaf over each, then cover and refrigerate for about 24 hours. Serve with ice cream.

Oranges Van der Hum

4 large or 6 medium, sweet, navel
oranges (about 800 g)
125 ml (½ cup) sugar
125 ml (½ cup) fresh orange juice
45 ml (3 Tbsp) Van der Hum liqueur

CANDIED ORANGE PEEL

Julienne the peel of 2 large oranges
(having removed all the white pith).
In a small saucepan, melt 60 ml
(4 Tbsp) sugar in 60 ml (¼ cup) water.
Add the orange strips and cook over
high heat until caramelised, then just
cover with cold water and a lid and
simmer slowly until soft. Leave to
cool; the juices will slowly be
absorbed. Sprinkle over the oranges
before serving.

Peel the oranges, remove all the white pith, and slice across into thin rings. Arrange in a flattish, heatproof dish – a 23–26 cm pie dish is ideal. Some slices will overlap, just squish them in gently until they're all lying flat. Spread the sugar out into a heavy, medium frying pan and allow to caramelise over low heat. You can stir occasionally just to spread it out, but mainly you should just shake the pan – it takes a while over low heat. Remove from the stove when it's a really deep toffee colour (no more, or it will scorch) and slowly and very carefully stir in the orange juice. The mixture will seize immediately, and make all sorts of weird tentacle-like shapes, but keep stirring and, if necessary put back on a low heat and stir until all the lumps have melted. Pour over the oranges, and then sprinkle the liqueur over evenly. Cool, cover and refrigerate for 2 days. Serve as is, or sprinkle with candied orange peel. **Serves 5–6 with ice cream.**

Spicy Poached Nectarines with Amarula Cream

If you make a large quantity – say triple the recipe – for a summer party (February being a good month for nectarines) and pile the poached fruit into a deep glass bowl set out on the table, a scary thought is that nobody will eat them because they look just too beautiful to disturb: smooth, round, glossy orange orbs. Gorgeous. The one disadvantage to this dessert is that for a successful result you need not just any old nectarine, but large clingstones, quite tart in flavour, with pinky-red skin and deep orange flesh, so you might have to shop around first – but a bonus is that it *has* to be made at least 24 hours in advance, so that the nectarines can soften and sweeten by soaking up the syrup.

500 ml (2 cups) water
125 ml (½ cup) sugar
1 fat stick cinnamon
1 ml (¼ tsp) freshly grated nutmeg
a squeeze of lemon juice
4 large nectarines (600–650 g)
8 whole cloves

AMARULA CREAM
For 4 nectarines, whip 125 ml (½ cup) fresh cream until stiff, then fold in 45 ml (3 Tbsp) Amarula. Now taste, you may want another tot. Chill until required.

Use a smallish, deep saucepan to take the fruit closely, and bring the water, sugar, cinnamon, nutmeg and lemon juice to the boil, stirring to dissolve the sugar, then leaving to simmer for about 5 minutes. In this time, pour boiling water over the nectarines, leave for about 30 seconds, then rinse under cold water and slip the skins off smoothly. Stick a clove into each side of each nectarine, then slide them into the syrup, reduce the heat, cover and poach gently for about 15 minutes, turning once, carefully. Before removing the fruit, do the skewer test: prick with a thin skewer – if it slips in easily right up to the pip, they're done. Using a slotted spoon, transfer to a small, deep bowl. Nick out the cloves – they've done their job – and boil the syrup rapidly until very bubbly and reduced by half, then strain over the nectarines. (The syrup will taste very sweet and concentrated at this stage – but it evens out on chilling.) Baste the nectarines a few times as they cool, then cover and refrigerate for 1–2 days. Serve 1 per diner, and pass the Amarula cream. **Serves 4.**

Pears in Phyllo Baskets with Sabayon

Baked custard has its place – and I, for one, love it – but there are times when you want to impress with a dessert that is a little smarter. Then this is it. The title may sound a little daunting, but the phyllo baskets are optional, and no step is either difficult or time-consuming to prepare.

about 750 g slightly underripe
Packham's Triumph pears
200 ml (⅘ cup) water
100 ml (⅖ cup) sugar
1 stick cinnamon
10 ml (2 tsp) fresh lemon juice
toasted almond flakes to decorate

SABAYON

3 XL free-range egg yolks
75 ml (5 Tbsp) sugar
5 ml (1 tsp) cornflour
45 ml (3 Tbsp) Amaretto liqueur
125 ml (½ cup) fresh cream

PHYLLO BASKETS

Brush large, deep muffin tins with butter and gently press in a square of phyllo, using only one layer. Brush lightly with melted butter, top with another square and brush with a little more butter. Bake at 200 C for about 5 minutes, until browned, then lift out of the tins and cool on a rack. If you wish, you can neaten the edges by snipping with kitchen scissors.

Peel, halve and core the pears. Bring the water, sugar, cinnamon and lemon juice to the boil in a wide-based pan, add the pears in a single layer, rounded sides up, cover and poach gently *just* until soft. Cool in the poaching liquid, then drain and chill. To make the sabayon, put the egg yolks, sugar and cornflour in the top of a small double boiler, or into a small saucepan set on top of a larger one and, using a balloon whisk, whisk until pale and thick. Keep the water simmering, *not* boiling, or the mixture will scramble; however it should not be undercooked either, or it will separate on standing. (This is the only tricky part.) Now slowly add the liqueur, and, using a wooden spoon, stir until the mixture thickens again – it should be creamy and butterscotch-coloured. Pour into a small container, cool, then refrigerate. Just before serving, whip the cream and fold it in. To serve, place one pear half, rounded side up, on each serving plate, or nestle it in a phyllo basket. Pour over enough of the sabayon to coat, sprinkle with almonds, and serve at once. **The sabayon is enough for 10–12 small pear halves.**

Poached Vanilla Peaches

If you use choice dessert peaches – Fairtime works well here – and if you poach them with a little wine added, together with a split vanilla pod – and if you serve them not only with vanilla ice cream, but with a small splash of *peach schnapps* over each OR the same of *caramelised verjuice syrup* – well, if you do all these things, you will (in my book) have a memorable dessert despite its simplicity. Or perhaps because of it.

250 ml (1 cup) water
60 ml (¼ cup) semi-sweet white wine
60 ml (4 Tbsp) vanilla sugar
1 large, soft vanilla pod, slit top to bottom
4 large, almost-ripe, free-stone dessert peaches (550 g)

Bring the water, wine, sugar and vanilla pod (scrape out the seeds, and include the pod) to the boil in a medium frying pan into which the peach halves will fit snugly, stirring to dissolve the sugar, then reduce the heat and leave to bubble gently while preparing the peaches as follows. Place in a bowl, cover with boiling water, leave to stand for about 30 seconds, then drain and run under cold water. Run a knife round each peach, vertically, just where the natural seam lies, then give a twist, the halves will separate and the skin should slip off easily, leaving you with eight, smooth as silk, brilliant orange peach halves. Submerge them in the syrup, rounded sides up, then cover and simmer gently for about 8 minutes or until tender, but *not pap*. Using a slotted spoon, transfer them to a heatproof pie dish (or something wide rather than deep), then boil the syrup rapidly until bubbly – 4–5 minutes. Strain over the peaches (dry the vanilla pod and store in sugar). The peaches should now lie bathed in a pinkish syrup speckled with fine vanilla seeds which managed to escape the sieve. Cool, then cover and refrigerate for a few hours. **Serves 4 doubles or 8 singles.**

Roasted Peaches

When peaches are in season it's tempting to serve them pure and fresh. There's something about sitting on a patio with peach juice dribbling down your chin that simply melts you with the joy of summer and sea and sun – but when a formal occasion demands that you fiddle with them a little in order to turn them into more of a dessert, then this is the answer. A quick paint and sprinkle beforehand, followed by a short bake – and out they come, soft and juicy and spattered with cinnamon, to be served hot with cream or ice cream, or at room temperature with a dollop of crème fraîche nestled in the hollows. Simple, but good.

4 large (500 g) ripe but unbruised free-stone peaches, e.g. Fairtime
melted butter
ground cinnamon
pale, runny honey
castor sugar

Pour boiling water over the peaches, leave to stand for 30 seconds, then run under cold water. Run a knife round the centres, vertically, twist and remove the stones, then slip off the skins and place, hollows up and close together, in a baking dish base-lined with baking paper. Brush each peach lightly with melted butter, then sprinkle with cinnamon (use your fingers, not a spoon, so that the cinnamon doesn't land in clumps). Drizzle a little honey over the cinnamon – about 2 ml (½ tsp) per peach is enough, and then sprinkle evenly with castor sugar – just a large pinch per peach should do, as they are sweet anyway. Bake, uncovered, at 200 C for 20–25 minutes until soft, speckled and juicy. Serve hot, or cool in the dish and serve at room temperature, but don't chill – the buttery juices will congeal. **Serves 4.**

Frozen Citrus Creams

You can buy such super ice creams these days that few of us bother to make them anymore. In any case, unless you have an ice-cream churn, or are willing to beat three times as it freezes, the texture is always a little grainy. The following lemon and orange creams are exceptions: smooth and refreshing and delicious. Serve them with anything, but a berry coulis would be good with the lemon and *Apricot Compote* with the orange.

Lemon

500 ml (2 cups) fresh cream
400 ml (1⅗ cups) sifted icing sugar
20 ml (4 tsp) very finely grated lemon rind
(2 large lemons)
6 XL free-range egg whites
5 ml (1 tsp) vanilla essence (or slightly less extract)

Whip the cream with the icing sugar and lemon rind until stiff. Whisk the egg whites until stiff (if you do this first you won't have to wash the beaters) and fold into the cream, with the vanilla. Use a metal spoon and fold in lightly, but combine the mixtures well. Pour into a 2-litre container and freeze quickly. Allow to soften for about 5 minutes before serving.

Orange

Exactly the same procedure as the lemon, but substitute 20 ml (4 tsp) very finely grated orange rind for the lemon. Walnuts are good with the orange flavour – add a handful, chopped, when folding in the egg whites.

Apricot Compote

Place the following in a small, heavy saucepan: 1 stick cinnamon; 1 whole star anise; ½ vanilla pod, split lengthwise; 125 ml (½ cup) fresh orange juice; 125 ml (½ cup) water; 2 ml (½ tsp) finely grated orange rind; 45 ml (3 Tbsp) light brown sugar. Bring to the boil, stirring to dissolve the sugar, then add 200 g soft, ready-to-eat dried apricots, reduce the heat, cover and simmer very gently for 12–15 minutes. Remove from the heat and stir in 15 ml (1 Tbsp) brandy. Cool and chill in a glass bowl overnight, but serve at room temperature – 2–3 plump apricots with some of the syrup per serving. Also good with chocolate ice cream. Muesli too.

Litchi & Amaretto Cheesecake

This old favourite refused to be left out for two good reasons: it's very big, and very delicious. It's also very rich – see note at the end.**

FILLING*

25 ml (5 tsp) gelatine

75 ml (5 Tbsp) water

3 XL free-range egg whites

200 ml (⅘ cup) castor sugar

1 x 250 g tub smooth, low-fat cottage cheese

250 g cream cheese**

60 ml (¼ cup) Amaretto liqueur

250 ml (1 cup) fresh cream

5 ml (1 tsp) vanilla essence

CRUST

Press a regular biscuit crust onto the base of a large, deep pie dish – 23 cm x 6 cm is just right. Don't do the sides, it's really unnecessary, and if you brush the base with a flavourless oil like canola, the slices will be easy to remove. Chill before adding the filling.

* Have all the ingredients, except the cream, at room temperature.

** For a slightly lower fat content use 500 g smooth, low-fat cottage cheese and omit the cream cheese.

Sponge the gelatine in the water, then dissolve over simmering water. Whisk the egg whites until fairly stiff, then gradually, while whisking, add *half* the sugar and whisk to a thick meringue. Without washing the beaters, whisk together the cheeses, remaining sugar and liqueur. When smooth, add the cream and vanilla and whip until the mixture thickens, then continue to whisk while you dribble in the dissolved gelatine. Fold in the meringue mixture, pour onto the crust and refrigerate until firm – it will set quickly.

For the topping, drain 1 x 565 g can pitted litchis, reserving the syrup. Pat the litchis dry, snip them into quarters and arrange on top of the cheesecake – do this best sides up – and don't worry if the entire top is not covered. Pour 100 ml (⅖ cup) of the reserved syrup into a small saucepan, stir in 7 ml (1½ tsp) cornflour, then bring to the boil, stirring, until clear and thick. Use a pastry brush to paint the litchis with dabs of this thick syrup – you won't need all of it, just enough to shine them up a bit. The finishing touch comes now: a sprinkling of toasted almond flakes. These complement the flavour and will also hide any bare patches. Return to the fridge until required. **Serves 10.**

Special Chocolate Bavarian Cream

A reasonably simple, alcohol-free, custard-based chocolate dessert set with gelatine might sound like a blancmange lifted from one of ouma's recipe books, but ouma did not use 70 per cent cocoa slabs – and this is what makes this one special. The eggs are in there, and so is the cream, along with a touch of coffee and cocoa powder – and the result is a dark, velvet-textured sweet finale that can be made the day before – a fact which is always comforting.

15 ml (1 Tbsp) gelatine (measure carefully, not a grain more)
10 ml (2 tsp) instant coffee granules dissolved in 60 ml (¼ cup) cold water
4 XL free-range eggs
150 ml (⅗ cup) sugar
10 ml (2 tsp) cornflour
600 ml (2⅖ cups) milk
30 ml (2 Tbsp) cocoa powder
2 x 100 g slabs dark 70 per cent cocoa chocolate (e.g. Belgian Intense)
400 ml (1⅗ cups) fresh cream
5 ml (1 tsp) vanilla essence

Sprinkle gelatine onto the cold coffee and leave to sponge. Whisk the eggs, sugar and cornflour until creamy. Scald the milk and cocoa, stir a little into the egg mixture, then pour the egg mixture into the saucepan and stir over low heat until the custard coats the back of a wooden spoon – it *must* thicken, but *must not* boil. Remove from the stove, add the sponged gelatine mixture, and stir until dissolved. Smear a small heatproof container with a dab of butter, add the chocolate, broken up roughly, and melt over simmering water. When just softened, scrape into the custard, give a quick whisk to make it absolutely smooth, then pour into a mixing bowl. Leave for a short while to cool and, when just beginning to thicken, whip the cream softly and fold in, with the vanilla. Pour into 10 glass goblets*, and set in the refrigerator**. A twirl of whipped cream would look attractive on the top of each, but as the dessert is rich as it is, a chocolate scroll or flake plunged into the middle would be a more elegant option. **Serves 10.**

* **May also be set in one large glass bowl if preferred.**
** **Keep refrigerated until just before serving.**

Butternut Pecan Pie

A soft and spicy mousse-like pie. Use a brilliant orange butternut, be lavish with the decoration, and enjoy a most unusual sweet ending.

CRUST

Line the base of a 20 x 6 cm pie dish with a biscuit crust – if handy, include a few ginger biscuit crumbs. Chill.

FILLING

12 ml (2½ tsp) gelatine

30 ml (2 Tbsp) cold water

500 g peeled and cubed butternut (prepared weight), preferably organic

2 ml (½ tsp) ground cinnamon

1 ml (¼ tsp) ground mixed spice

60 ml (4 Tbsp) sugar

15 ml (1 Tbsp) golden syrup

2 XL free-range eggs, separated

10 ml (2 tsp) cornflour

60 ml (¼ cup) milk

125 ml (½ cup) fresh cream

2 ml (½ tsp) vanilla essence

pecan halves, preserved ginger and ground cinnamon for topping

Sprinkle the gelatine onto the water and leave to sponge. Boil the butternut in a *little* lightly salted water until soft. Drain if necessary and cool down before whizzing in a blender until smooth. You should have 500 ml (2 cups) thick puré. Spoon into a heavy saucepan and add the spices, sugar, syrup and the egg yolks beaten with the cornflour and milk. Stir over low heat until the mixture becomes very thick, like a dense, cooked custard, but be careful not to boil. Remove from the heat and immediately stir in the sponged gelatine, continuing to stir until dissolved. Cool the mixture in a mixing bowl and, when cold but not set, fold in the cream softly whipped with the vanilla, followed by the egg whites, whisked until stiff but not dry – stir a spoonful through the mixture and fold in the rest. Pour onto the biscuit crust and refrigerate until firm, then top with the pecans, snip over a knob or two of the ginger and finish with a very fine dusting of cinnamon. **Makes 8 wedges.**

Lemon Meringue

If you put the meringue at the bottom and the lemon filling on top, you avoid the pitfall of a weepy meringue pie. This is a fairly tart tart — not too sweet, and refreshingly lemony. If you prefer a fruity, cream-filled filling, try one of the variations, which you could also use to fill a pavlova. Or double the quantities for the meringue shell and make two (use a large baking tray so that they bake on the same oven shelf), then fill the extra one with one of the alternative fillings.

MERINGUE

2 XL free-range egg whites (at room temperature)

a pinch of salt

a pinch of cream of tartar

125 ml (½ cup) castor sugar

LEMON FILLING

2 XL free-range egg yolks

30 ml (2 Tbsp) fresh lemon juice

2 ml (½ tsp) finely grated lemon rind

60 ml (4 Tbsp) castor sugar

125 ml (½ cup) milk

20 ml (4 tsp) cornflour

125 ml (½ cup) fresh cream

2 ml (½ tsp) vanilla essence

toasted almond flakes for topping

To make the meringue shell, whisk the egg whites until foamy. Add the salt and cream of tartar and whisk until stiff. Gradually add the castor sugar, whisking constantly until the mixture becomes very thick and glossy. Shape the meringue into a 20 cm circle on a baking tray lined with two sheets of baking paper – do not grease anything, and use a regular-type tray, not a coated one. (To secure the paper, use a dollop of meringue below each corner.) Using a spoon, gently flatten the centre and pull the sides inwards to form a rim. Bake at 150 C for 15 minutes, then at 120 C for 1 hour. Switch off the oven and leave the shell – even overnight – until absolutely cold.

For the lemon filling, whisk together the yolks, lemon juice and rind, castor sugar, milk and cornflour, pour into a heavy-based saucepan and stir over very low heat until cooked – like a thick custard. Leave to cool, stirring occasionally to prevent a skin from forming. Whip the cream with the vanilla, give the custard a quick whisk to make sure it's absolutely smooth, then fold it into the cream in small dollops. Pour into the meringue shell, spreading evenly, sprinkle with the almonds, and refrigerate until firm. **Makes 6 wedges.**

Passion Meringue

Some people dislike passion fruit (granadilla) pips. They think they have lost a filling. Try the following variation, which uses only the juice, with fresh mango and thick cream. Ingredients are easily doubled to fill a larger shell.

PASSION FRUIT FILLING

3–4 large, ripe passion fruit, halved

125 ml (½ cup) fresh cream

15 ml (1 Tbsp) icing sugar

1 ripe mango (300 g), peeled and cut into small cubes

Hold the passion fruit halves over a small strainer and squeeze hard until you have 30–40 ml (6–8 tsp) juice. Whip the cream with the icing sugar, add the juice and whip until very stiff, then fold in the mango. Pile the filling into the shell, and serve, or refrigerate for a few hours if working ahead.

No decoration is needed, as the flavour is delicate and should be left to speak for itself – although, having said that, the juice (and pips) of just one granadilla will enhance the appearance. **Makes 6 wedges.**

Strawberry Meringue

Ingredients are easily doubled for a large meringue shell. Other fruits such as bananas could, of course, be added, but there's something very summery and delicious about a pure strawberry meringue.

STRAWBERRY FILLING

250 g ripe, red strawberries

5 ml (1 tsp) castor sugar

5 ml (1 tsp) balsamic vinegar

125 ml (½ cup) fresh cream

15 ml (1 Tbsp) icing sugar

20 ml (4 tsp) Amaretto liqueur*

a few drops of vanilla essence

Rinse and hull strawberries and slice enough of them into fairly small pieces to fill 250 ml (1 cup) or measure 150 g in weight. Reserve the remaining berries for decoration. Place the sliced berries in a single layer on a large plate and sprinkle over the castor sugar and vinegar. Leave for about 20 minutes, then pour off the juices that will have drawn. Whip the cream with the icing sugar, liqueur and vanilla, fold in the berries, spoon into the meringue shell, decorate with the remaining berries and serve or refrigerate briefly. **Makes 6 wedges.**

* This may seem very little, and more can be added to taste, but be careful not to make the cream runny.

Apple & Mango Crumble

There's hardly a fruit that hasn't been turned into a crumble, for the simple reason that when it comes to homespun, comforting desserts, crumbles are probably top of the list. The following is another variation on the theme, with mango and coconut introducing a tropical touch, and cashews adding crunch.

1 x 765 g can unsweetened pie apple slices
1 x 410 g can mango slices, drained and syrup reserved
30 ml (2 Tbsp) golden syrup
30 ml (2 Tbsp) sugar

CRUMBLE
375 ml (1½ cups) cake flour
5 ml (1 tsp) baking powder
a small pinch of sea salt
7 ml (1½ tsp) ground cinnamon
90 ml (6 Tbsp) castor sugar (or vanilla sugar if available)
90 ml (6 Tbsp) desiccated coconut
100 g butter
cashew nuts, halved or roughly chopped

If the apples are in large slices, chop into chunks. Chop the mango slices too. Place in a buttered 23 x 5 cm pie dish, pour over 125 ml (½ cup) of the reserved mango syrup, and mix in the golden syrup and sugar. To make the crumble, place the flour, baking powder, salt and cinnamon in a processor fitted with the metal blade and pulse to mix, then add the castor sugar and coconut, pulse again, then add the butter and pulse until the mixture is finely crumbed. Sprinkle this over the fruit – it will be thickly covered – and finish with a scatter of cashews. Bake at 180 C for 45 minutes until the crumble is toast-coloured and the syrup is bubbling through. Serve warm, rather than hot, with thick cream. **Serves 6–8.**

* If you'd prefer a more wholesome topping, mix 250 ml (1 cup) unsweetened muesli with 125 ml (½ cup) self-raising flour, 30 g chopped pecan nuts, 5 ml (1 tsp) ground cinnamon, 90 ml (6 Tbsp) light brown sugar and 125 ml (½ cup) oil.

Orange Bavarois with Hot Chocolate Sauce

Everything here can be done in advance, making this an ideal dessert when entertaining. The hot dark sauce drizzled over the chilled little puddings is both colourful and delicious, and the addition of egg whites lightens the traditional rich bavarois-type custard, making the flavour very delicate.

15 ml (1 Tbsp) gelatine
125 ml (½ cup) fresh orange juice
375 ml (1½ cups) milk
finely grated rind of 1 medium orange
2 XL free-range eggs, separated
60 ml (4 Tbsp) castor sugar
a small pinch of salt
a few drops of vanilla essence
125 ml (½ cup) fresh cream,
softly whipped

SAUCE

Melt 100 g broken up plain milk chocolate (not white, nor dark) with 30 ml (2 Tbsp) pouring cream and 30 ml (2 Tbsp) milk in a small double boiler or saucepan over low heat. Stir occasionally until smooth – do not allow to boil or bubble. It may now be set aside and gently reheated, with 20–30 ml (4–6 tsp) Van der Hum liqueur (optional) added just before serving.

Sprinkle the gelatine onto the orange juice and leave to sponge. Scald the milk with the orange rind – do this over low heat, in order to release all the orange flavour. Whisk the egg yolks with the castor sugar until pale and thick. Using a fine sieve, slowly strain the hot milk onto the egg mixture, stir to mix, add a pinch of salt, then return to the saucepan and cook as for custard over very low heat, stirring, until the mixture coats the back of a wooden spoon. It has to thicken, but dare not boil. Remove from the stove, stir in the sponged gelatine and vanilla, give a quick whisk to make sure that all the gelatine has dissolved, then cool in a mixing bowl. Hurry this up by standing the mixing bowl in a bowl of cold water. Once cooled, it may be chilled briefly until just thickening, but not yet setting. Fold in the cream, and then the stiffly whisked egg whites – use a metal spoon and stir a spoonful through the mixture first, then fold in the remainder. Pour into eight rinsed ramekins (about 6 cm diameter, 5 cm deep) and refrigerate until set. Overnight, if you wish.

Unmould the ramekins onto serving plates by running a knife round the sides and giving a gentle shake. Drizzle a little of the hot sauce over each, allowing it to run down the sides. **Serves 8.**

Creamy Rummy Fruit Salad with Crunchy Pecans

I think seriously rich desserts are a fabulous treat in a restaurant because eating out is (usually) an occasional treat, but I don't like making a habit of serving them at home. I once saw a guest hide her incredibly rich but utterly superb (I didn't make it) chocolate terrine behind the dining-room curtain at the back of her chair, because she was full after two spoonfuls, but did not want to offend her hostess. It's true. And that's one of the reasons why I like serving a fruit salad – tart it up, give it a fancy name, and everyone can finish it. Tropical fruits are the best.

4 mangoes (about 1.1 kg), peeled and cubed
4 bananas, sliced and tossed in lemon juice
400 g peeled and cubed papino (prepared weight)
12–16 fresh or canned litchis, pitted and slivered
150 ml (⅗ cup) thick, low-fat Bulgarian yoghurt
150 ml (⅗ cup) crème fraîche
30 ml (2 Tbsp) pale, runny honey (fynbos is a good choice)
30 ml (2 Tbsp) dark rum

TOPPING
30 ml (2 Tbsp) soft brown sugar
15 ml (1 Tbsp) butter
30 ml (2 Tbsp) water
about 125 ml (½ cup) pecan nut halves or quarters

Mix all the fruit gently in a beautiful glass bowl – wide, rather than deep. Mix the remaining ingredients; don't whisk, just stir until smoothly combined, then pour over the fruit, cover and refrigerate for 3–4 hours.

For the topping, melt the sugar and butter in the water in a small pan over low heat. Add the pecans and toss until crunchy. Drain on a paper towel, set aside, and sprinkle over the fruit salad just before serving. **Serves 8–10.**

Orange Liqueur Chocolate Truffles

Instead of a dessert, pass these round after the cheese and biscuits as a sweet finale.

75 ml (5 Tbsp) cream

2 ml (½ tsp) very finely grated orange rind

100 g dark chocolate, broken into small pieces

5 ml (1 tsp) butter

15 ml (1 Tbsp) orange liqueur (Van der Hum is fine)

cocoa powder for coating

Scald the cream with the orange rind – it should be very hot, but not boiling. Remove from the heat, add the chocolate and stir until melted – if this takes too long, you can return it briefly to the stove plate (turned off) and give a quick stir. Remove and mix in the butter and orange liqueur, then scrape into a small bowl. Leave to cool completely – about 30 minutes, but it does depend on the weather – and then, using an electric whisk, whisk on high speed until the mixture becomes paler and shiny. Refrigerate until firm enough to handle – at least 2 hours. Use a teaspoon to scoop into balls, and roll around on a plate liberally dusted with cocoa powder. If the mixture is a little sticky, coat your palms with cocoa as well. Keep refrigerated, but don't serve icy cold. **Makes 12.**

Baked Apple Puff

... or Ouma's Winter Fruit Cobbler. A hearty, homespun pudding, large and sweet and easy to make. Serve warm, rather than hot, with whipped cream or home-made custard.

1 x 765 g can unsweetened pie apple slices*
2 large bananas OR 2 large fresh pears OR 1 of each
125 ml (½ cup) golden syrup
100 ml (⅖ cup) hot water
60 ml (4 Tbsp) seedless raisins
250 ml (1 cup) self-raising flour
7 ml (1½ tsp) ground cinnamon
2 ml (½ tsp) freshly grated nutmeg
90 ml (6 Tbsp) light brown sugar**
90 ml (6 Tbsp) desiccated coconut
250 ml (1 cup) oil
2 XL free-range eggs
a pinch of salt

Chop the apples into smaller pieces. Dice the bananas, and peel, core and dice the pears. Mix the apples and chosen fruit, and spoon into a lightly buttered 23 cm pie dish, at least 6 cm deep (or the syrup will bubble over). Melt the golden syrup in the water and pour over the fruit. Sprinkle in the raisins. Whisk the remaining ingredients together to make a thick batter, then simply drop in spoonfuls over the fruit – the batter will spread during baking. Bake at 180 C for 35–40 minutes until the topping is lightly browned and firm. Remove from the oven very carefully as the syrup will be bubbling. Allow to cool down a little before serving. **Serves 8.**

* **Use choice-grade pie apples, firmly packed, with no juice to speak of.**
** **90 ml, which equals 6 Tbsp, is easily measured if you use an 83 ml metric cup and add on 7 ml (half a metric tablespoon).**

Chocolate Fudge Cups

If you're a reluctant dessert maker, the answer is to buy some stunning, small espresso or after-dinner coffee cups. Desserts will stretch amazingly when all they have to do is fill a small cup. Another bonus is that desserts that come in coffee cups are usually rich and quick to make – like the following serious chocolate fixes.

butter

100 g dark chocolate, broken up*

5 ml (1 tsp) cocoa powder

250 ml (1 cup) fresh cream

2 ml (½ tsp) vanilla essence

15 ml (1 Tbsp) icing sugar

chocolate shavings for sprinkling – use white chocolate, plain brown or dark

Smear a very small saucepan with a little butter (this makes it easier to scrape out). Add the chocolate, cocoa and 50 ml (⅕ cup) of the cream. Melt over very low heat, stirring a few times just to get it going. Remove from the heat as soon as the mixture is smooth, and set aside until completely cool, but not firm. Whip the remaining cream with the vanilla and icing sugar until thick but not stiff, then slowly whisk in the cooled chocolate mixture in dollops – make about five additions altogether, and stop as soon as everything is smoothly combined and uniformly chocolate in colour. Spoon into five or six little cups**, sprinkle with chocolate and place in the coldest part of the fridge – it should be softly set in about 2 hours, or less. **Serves 5–6, and is easily doubled.**

* You may find a guest putting one of these behind the curtain (see Creamy Rummy Fruit Salad with Crunchy Pecans, page 170), but if you *really* want a denser, darker, even richer fix, use 125–150 g chocolate. The flavour will be very intense, with a firmer texture.
** For Chocolate Meringue, smooth the mixture into a baked meringue shell (see page 168) and refrigerate to set.

Estrelita

Estrelita marched down the main street of Corriebush in a few ostrich feathers and little else. The rest of the troupe were modestly dressed in bright satin blouses, floral waistcoats and bell-bottomed trousers. But Estrelita was their star, their finest performer, and with her toned, lithe body and flamboyant personality she was quite the best advertisement for the circus. With Estrelita at the head of the procession, wiggling her hips, twirling her feathers and flashing mischievous invitations to all those watching, they could be sure of a full house at every performance.

Not that there was any danger of empty seats in Corriebush. Ever since the advertisement in the *Corriebush Daily* announcing a visit by the Circus Olé, the whole town had been in a fever.

'Have you seen what's *coming*?' Anna enthused over tea.

Of course they had.

'The tent is already up, on the field next to the rugby grounds.'

'There'll be acrobats and tight-rope walkers and ladies in boxes, sawn clean in half!'

'Herman likes the fire-eaters,' said Lily.

'Daniel likes the clowns.'

'And I,' said Sophia, 'like the flying men in tights. You can see *everything*. Just like bunches of grapes.'

'Sophia!'

The Circus Olé gave three performances, and the six friends went to every one, making sure that they arrived early in order to secure ringside seats. The circus folk loved them, because they reacted so gustily to all the scary moments. When the fire-eater pretended to throw his flaming torch into the audience they ducked their heads and screamed. When the strong man advanced towards Amelia, making as if to scoop her up, she shouted 'Ag no man!' and ran to the entrance. They laughed so much at the clowns that Nellie bounced right off her chair onto the grass, and had to be helped back up.

And when Estrelita feigned a slip on the high trapeze, letting the cross-bar dangle into space without her, Maria rushed forward, arms outstretched, to catch her in case she fell. In the end they were all peeping through their fingers, afraid of witnessing a disaster, but reluctant to miss a single spine-chilling moment.

At the end of the final performance they stood up and clapped for so long that the ringmaster had to signal them to stop.

'I have an announcement,' he said, turning in circles as he spoke so that everyone could hear him. 'It is with great sadness that tonight we are bidding farewell to Estrelita.'

The audience groaned in dismay. 'Ag no, not Estrelita!' The ringmaster held up his hand.

'It's sad news for us, but good news for Corriebush!'

Puzzled, they glanced at each other. 'Yes, you lucky people! Estrelita has decided to stay here for a while. She needs to work on a new routine, and to have a rest from travelling. She has chosen to spend her sabbatical here in Corriebush because she has been so impressed by the beauty of the town and the friendliness of its people.' A happy murmur rippled through the tent. 'We'll leave her caravan in the Park, and I know you will welcome her with open hearts.' Estrelita stepped forward and bowed down so low that her feathers fell right over her head, a sight that prompted Servaas to whistle so loudly through his teeth that he almost lost them. Then she waved to the crowd, hugged the ringmaster, and waltzed into her dressing room.

The following morning the friends gathered on Lily's stoep. There had been no pre-arrangement. They instinctively recognised the need for a meeting over tea, and arrived one by one: Amelia, Nellie, Anna, Sophia and Maria, all in a twitter, for there was much to be discussed. What lay ahead was not simply a tea party with scones, as was so often the case in their predictable lives. On this particular morning there was News.

Lily wasted no time. 'A star has descended in our midst.'

'Right out of the blue,' went on Sophia.

'We need to treat her with great respect.'

'Kid gloves, as they say.'

'Point is, she has chosen to stay with us, so we must be sure not to intrude on her privacy in any way.'

'And yet we have to make her feel welcome, but because she's not like other people we can't really call on her with tea and scones.'

'Has to watch her figure.'

'And work on her new routine.'

'She will also have to practise.'

'I wonder what she will actually *do*?'

What Estrelita actually did was to take to the trees.

Lily watched in silent amazement from her front stoep, but by the third morning could not contain herself any longer, so she trotted over with a tray.

'Yoo-hoo!' she called. 'I'm Lily and I've brought a little something for your breakfast because I haven't seen you shop or anything. Don't you get very hungry, flying around like that all day?'

Estrelita ran over to her. 'This is just paradise! The fresh air, and the birds and the sun and the freedom … I can do what I like, whenever I like,' and she did a quick backward somersault to illustrate her joy.

Then she accepted the tray with its flask of coffee and plate of *beskuit*, kissed Lily on the cheek, waved and was gone.

Lily started taking her a tray every morning, not only because she was kind, but also because she loved to watch the performance. Early morning, even before sunrise, was Estrelita's time for keeping in shape. Hair flying, sometimes whooping with happiness, she stood on the swings, pumping so hard that she would whoosh clean over the top and back to earth again; she hung upside down on the jungle gym and twisted her head between her legs; she stood on the grass and did eight somersaults in a row, forward and back, then she lodged her right foot behind her left ear. She always gratefully accepted Lily's breakfast, then retired to her caravan to plan her next routines.

And then suddenly one morning Sophia's husband Dawid appeared. Dawid was the caretaker and very proud of his Park. Certainly, he had seen the caravan standing there, but as he had attended the circus performance he knew all about Estrelita, and he was happy for her to be with them. But one morning it came to him while sipping his first cup of coffee, that her caravan was going to kill the grass if it stood in one spot all the time. So he decided to go over and ask her whether he and some of his mates could move

it a little to the right, in order to give the lawn a chance. Sophia said she was sure Estrelita would understand. 'Go now, before she starts her day,' she suggested. 'We're being very careful not to meddle with her programme.'

Dawid reached the gate to the Park and stopped dead. Estrelita was in the middle of a major session, in which she was testing appallingly risky manoeuvres that she had devised the previous day.

On this particular morning she was not merely flitting from branch to branch of the oak trees, she was sailing into space in a glorious whirl of strong brown limbs and purple tights, flying with fistfuls of leaves in her hands, pelting from one tree to the

next, taking impossible gaps and shaving past the massive trunks with just millimetres to spare. As he stood there watching, trails of sweat started slowly snaking down Dawid's chest under his shirt, and his heart began to thrum alarmingly, so he went home.

'What, back so soon?' exclaimed Sophia. Usually, he was away for quite a while each morning. His job as caretaker of Parks and Other Amenities included putting up the nets on the tennis courts, checking on the state of the water furrows and feeding the two small monkeys who were the sole inhabitants of the town Zoo. These duties usually took him until just before morning tea.

'*Ja-nee*,' he answered, staring thoughtfully into his mug of steaming coffee.'

'You look a little pale, Dawid. Is there something wrong in the Park, then?'

'No, no. Nothing serious. But I'll have to check up again tomorrow morning.'

Dawid 'checked up' on six consecutive mornings, and on the seventh he nailed a sign to the gate. It read: 'As From Henceforth No High Jinks In The Park. By Law.'

The women were astonished, and questioned Sophia.

'Why has Dawid put up that sign?' they wanted to know. 'What about Estrelita?'

Sophia was ready. 'He says it's him who is responsible to the council for any accidents and he can't stand it any longer, looking at a major one just waiting to happen, with her flashing all over the place like Tarzan. His nerves are quite on the loose, he says, and so he's thinking of resigning.'

'*Ag* no, he's such a good caretaker.'

'Perhaps it's the skimpy leotard that's giving him the jitters.'

'Never! Not my Dawid! He's just doing his job.'

'But if she can't practise what will she do?'

'We'll think of a plan.'

And they did. The very next day they called on Estrelita, all six of them, with a bunch of flowers and a roast chicken, all fat and skin removed. They sat themselves down round the small kitchen table, and explained the position.

Estrelita was astonished. She had not even noticed the sign, which was on a gate behind her caravan, so the fact that her presence was causing a problem came as a nasty shock. Lily noticed the tears gathering, so she hurried on.

'But don't worry, Essie, we have a grand idea.' She paused to give her words greater impact. 'You are going to open a gym!'

Anxiously the women leant forward, elbows on the table, desperately hoping that she would approve their plan. She did not disappoint them.

'A gym! You mean a place with bicycles and mats and balls and bars?' They nodded, smiling with relief.

'I've *always* longed to be an instructor,' she said, 'with ladies exercising to music, firming and toning everything, and men working their muscles and flattening their stomachs! But the money? I'll have to hire a hall and buy all the equipment and a gramophone and records and …'

'Never you worry, *liefie*. We have a little money box, and every time we have tea together, we pop in a few coins for emergencies. And this is an emergency, not so?' Maria looked round the table and they all nodded. 'Of course.'

'That's settled then. Just make a list of what you need and I'll place an order with a man I know in Port Elizabeth. He's a life-saver on Humewood Beach, and so he knows everything about muscles and keeping fit.'

'And the hall?'

'Dawid will sort that out,' promised Sophia. 'Seeing he started the whole affair. In any case, as a caretaker he has his finger on all the pies. He'll find something vacant at a reasonable rental or my name's not Sophia Aspidistra Joubert née O'Connor.'

Within a fortnight the whole show was up and running, and nearly all the inhabitants of Corriebush had put their names down as members. Estrelita had, in the meantime, worked out a gentle aerobics routine for the women, and a more vigorous one for the men. 'Gets rid of the paunches and blows up the biceps. Just wait and see.'

Classes for the women were to be held in the mornings, men in the afternoons. On the first morning they arrived punctually at nine, in their patio pants and loose floral blouses. Estrelita put on a Strauss waltz, gave each a huge, inflated ball and told the women to lie on them, like slabs of steak, and then lift their arms out sideways like an aeroplane.

Sophia fell off immediately. 'Oh my glory.'

'Use your stomach muscles and don't lift your head.'

She climbed back on and the ball popped out sideways.

'*Ag* no. This is not what balls are for.'

'Sophia!'

'Right then, we'll start with the easy stuff. Stand on your mats and drop your heads to the floor.' They all hung there like pyramids.

'Now slowly stand erect, pinching your crotches to your navels and dropping your shoulders down to your hips as you *slowly* stand up, one vertebra at a time.'

The women unrolled, exclaiming and puffing, until they eventually, triumphantly, stood erect.

'Now suck your navels into your spines.'

'Excuse me?'

'Look down. Do you see your stomachs?'

Yes, they all saw their stomachs.

'Now suck them in until you can see your toes.'

So, looking down, they took huge, deep breaths which made their chests swell up and their faces turn red. Alarmed, Estrelita turned on the fan.

'Perhaps we should start with arms and weights. We don't have any dumbbells, so I've brought along cans of baked beans. Now, one in each hand, lift your right arms in line with your right shoulders.'

She walked round the room, stopping to wiggle the loose flesh women carry on their underarms. 'See that? It's got to go.'

She squeezed the soft folds below their shoulder blades. 'That too.'

She moved down and pinched their waists.

'*Eina!*'

'Just as I thought. Not a bone in sight. Come ladies, we have a lot of work to do.'

Of all the women in Estrelita's class, the six friends worked the hardest. They never missed a session. They also never missed their tea parties afterwards, usually on Lily's stoep. 'We deserve it,' they reasoned, munching happily. Not surprisingly, they did not lose any weight. Every Saturday morning they met at the chemist shop, where there was a large scale. One by one they stepped onto the platform, inserted a coin into the slot, and watched as the needle shot up on the dial.

'*Ag* no!' Naïvely, they were always disappointed, and complained to Estrelita.

'But ladies! Just look at the centimetres you have lost!' She fetched a tape measure. Between them they had lost a total of over a metre.

'Forget the scale, just look at your waists!'

They looked.

'Your thighs! Your buttocks! Your upper arms!'

Suddenly, unexpectedly, they were shy. They stopped inspecting themselves; rather, they turned to look each other up and down.

It was true. They were all slimmer, trimmer, and glowing.

And so were their men.

'You should just see Daniels's stomach. Flat as a puncture.'

'And Servaas' thighs! In shorts, from the back, they're amazing.'

'I wonder what she does with them?'

'Servaas' thighs?'

'*Ag* no. What she does with the men to tone them up so much?'

'No baked beans and rubber balls. It must be really tough stuff. Perhaps we should pop in one afternoon and see?'

Sophia did.

And what she saw was Dawid lying on his back on the floor, with Estrelita

sitting astride him, her hands on his chest, her face on his face. Sophia screamed. 'Dawid, what the *blerrie* blazes are you doing?'

'Right now he's not doing anything, Sophia,' Daniel told her. 'He's not even breathing.'

Daniel tried to steer her out. 'It's not what you're thinking, Sophia.'

'How do you know what I'm thinking?' Sophia snapped, scratching in her handbag for a handkerchief.

Dawid was rushed to the local hospital and immediately to the operating room, where Dr Ackermann saw him and decided that an operation was not necessary. 'He's had a fairly severe heart attack, though and should stay here for at least two weeks.' Then he turned to Estrelita, who had refused to wait in the corridor. 'I must congratulate you,' he smiled. 'Without a doubt you saved his life.'

Sophia visited Dawid every day, sitting at his bedside with a basketful of gifts: little bunches of violets and sweet-peas, packets of fudge, long ropes of biltong and cans of beer which, as soon as she had left, the nurses confiscated. Estrelita also visited every day, and the two women often found themselves there at the same time. Gradually an intimate friendship developed.

Sophia, who so often chattered and blustered and spoke without thinking, suddenly showed another side to her nature. Dawid's illness seemed to have calmed her down, made her less ebullient and more thoughtful. She took a gentle, sincere interest in Estrelita and, without any rude probing, egged her on to talk about herself, her childhood, her life in the circus. They talked for hours, sitting one on either side of Dawid's bed, keeping their voices low so as not to disturb him.

A strange story started to unravel.

'My name is not really Estrelita. That's just my circus name. I was christened Magdalena – my parents called me Maggie – and we lived on a farm near Nelspruit. My father didn't actually own it, he was only an assistant manager to the boss, so we didn't have much money and until I was twelve I went to the farm school, which was free. But then my *Oupa* said he would pay for me to go to boarding school because all I was learning on the farm was how to climb trees.'

Sophia felt she should say something. '*Ag siestog!*'

'I hated school. They put me in Standard Two, with all the little children, and even then I failed. I was only happy on the sports field, and when I won a silver cup for hurdles and another for high-jump, my *Oupa* took me to the circus as a reward.'

'And that was the start of it all?'

'The start of it all.'

There were several circuses touring the country at that time, and whenever they visited Nelspruit, Estrelita would beg to be taken. Her *Oupa* never refused his granddaughter, because every year she won more silver cups – hurdles, high-jump, bar-work in the gym, and he was very proud of her. He knew, too, that she was also working at her studies, because her report cards were improving. But what he did not know was that, when a circus was in town she would slip out of the hostel every afternoon after games, and run down to the Big Top.

'It was the smell of the sawdust, I inhaled it like a perfume. The sawdust and the canvas tent and the smell of painted faces and grease, and I would sit down, just inside the open flap, and watch them practising, day after day. I loved all the circuses, but Olé was my favourite. One afternoon, when they were having their tea break, I found myself walking into the ring – it was like in a dream, when your legs move on their own – and I walked to where the rope was dangling, and I climbed it – right up, to the platform at the top. Then I started swinging in small circles, one leg on the platform, one hand on the rope.'

Sophia clapped her hand to her forehead. '*Sjoe* child! What happened then?'

'They came back from their tea break and saw me, and Carmella – their trapeze artist – shinned up the rope to where I was standing. 'Oh, but she looked so beautiful in her bra and silver tights!'

Dawid suddenly opened his eyes. 'What was that?' he asked faintly. Sophia jumped. 'Go to sleep Dawid, you're not supposed to talk yet, nor breathe.'

'And she didn't scold,' Estrelita continued, 'she just smiled at me and told me to follow her down. "And when you reach the ground," she said, "I want you to do the splits and two backward somersaults." And I did. Then she asked me to come back the next day. I was so excited that I skipped assembly and got there while they were still having breakfast.

'The manager found me sitting in my usual place. "Ah! There you are!" he called. "Carmella has told me about you." Then he held out his hand, pulled me to my feet and guided me into his office, where he waved me to a chair, pulled out a notepad and said he wanted to ask me a few questions.

'It seemed to me like an eternity before he finally came to the point.

'He leaned back in his chair, twiddled his pencil, and said "We think, Maggie, that you have a talent that's worth developing, and we would like to offer you the chance of joining us for a trial period. You won't be paid, but you will have free instruction, board and lodging.

"It's important that your parents should be happy about this. What do you think?" I truly did not know, but I told him that they would not mind, because I was nearly eighteen and about to leave school. And that my *Oupa* would be very proud.'

'And your parents really didn't mind?'

'Well, they were a bit shocked at first, but I begged them to give me a chance. And of course *Oupa* was on my side. He said, "Let Maggie give it a try. Six months and then we'll talk again. And we'll go together to meet the manager and make sure that he'll take extra special care of her." I went the following week.'

'My goodness child, so *that's* how it all started! Did they ever come to see you perform?'

'The night of my first appearance in Nelspruit they were sitting in the front row. I was very nervous, but everything went really well, and when I had finished my act the audience clapped and clapped and the clowns carried me round the ring on their shoulders. It was that night that I was given the name Estrelita and then I knew, really knew, that this was where I wanted to be, to use my body, to work at my acts, and to be a part of that circus family forever.'

'Well, now just think of that,' said Sophia, feeling all choked up, which frequently happened when she was happy. But then the old Sophia broke loose and blundered on.

'Tell me now, what about boyfriends, *liefie?* A pretty girl like you! You can't make whoopee with a rope, after all.'

'Sophia!'

'Go to sleep, Dawid.'

'Why aren't you married yet? I mean, living with all those strong men doing clever tricks and looking like film stars? Just like my favourite, Cary Grant. I once asked two of them straight out – I said, "Are You Perhaps Cary Grant?"'

Estrelita smiled her famous, radiant smile. 'Yes, believe it or not, my man is just as handsome. Even has a dimple in his chin.'

'So?'

'Well, he's my very special boyfriend, and I want to marry him, but he's not quite sure – so that's actually why I am taking this break in Corriebush – to give him time to think things through.'

'But what's the *blerrie* matter with him then? A lovely lady like you, and he has to first *think* about it?'

Estrelita took a while to answer. 'He's in a wheelchair.'

'*Ag* no.'

'Juan was our best male trapeze artist and he had a fall and injured his spine. The doctors who examined him said they didn't know if he would ever walk again, and he said we both needed time to think because now everything had changed, and he could not expect it of me. Well, I *have* thought it through very carefully, and my mind is made up. He's the man I want to spend my life with. I'm simply waiting for the circus's next visit next week – he's still with them working as the cashier, taking tickets and money – and then I'll tell him.'

The wedding ceremony took place in the Town Hall. The whole town was invited and Sophia was matron of honour, in pale pink chiffon, with her hair swept up, secured with a pearl pin and a pink rose. She looked delightful, and Dawid was well enough to attend the ceremony and smile his approval.

Juan, of course, was in his wheelchair. Estrelita stood by his side. She wore a full-length blue dress and a soft blue feather in her hair.

The six friends catered, the champagne flowed, and everyone sang *Hasta Mañna* , which they had been practising for days.

The following morning Juan went into hospital. Corriebush was a small town, but the hospital and doctors were respected throughout the Province. Their prognosis was that there was every hope, but that he would need at least two operations. The vertebra were cracked, they said, but not crushed, and he could be walking within a year. Not for sure, but very probably.

The day Juan came out of the hospital, they were waiting, and a cheer went up as Herman wheeled him out through the double doors and down the ramp, followed by a smiling Estrelita.

Dawid stepped forward.

'I speak on behalf of all the inhabitants of Corriebush,' he began, but got no further.

'You must think us very rude,' said Lily.

'You've had to wait so long,' Nellie went on.

'The reason is, it wasn't ready,' explained Anna.

'But we think you'll like it!' beamed Sophia.

The couple were beginning to look very bemused, so Daniel took over.

'It's your wedding present,' and he handed them a large white envelope.

Estrelita and Juan opened it together, both trembling a little. Perhaps they were expecting a cheque, which would have embarrassed them both. Or a poem, or something to make them cry. But it was none of these things.

They slit the top and pulled out a large brass key. Puzzled, Juan held it up. 'A key?'

'*Ja*, a key. Our gift to you: a renovated little cottage in Corriebush. It's yours.'

Neither of them could speak, so one by one their friends helped out.

'You see, Juan needs to be here. For the doctors.'

'And you, Estrelita, need to be here. For us.'

'We need you to keep us on our toes.'

'Heads up, backs straight.'

'Stomachs in.'

'And navels to spine.'

'Now off you go. You'll know the cottage by the name on the gate.'

It read simply: OLÉ!

Baking

Florrie's Fruitcake

It's one of those well-known, flop-proof boiled fruitcakes, but somehow this one is special: heavy with fruit and nuts and cherries, it weighs between 1 kg and 1.5 kg and, as it is not a very thick cake, it can easily take a layer of marzipan and icing and become a last-minute Christmas cake. On the other hand, if you would rather have it plain, the mixture is stiff enough to support halved cherries, decoratively arranged on the top before baking. If you want a deeper, 'fatter' cake, use a 20 cm tin, but bake for *slightly* longer.

500 g fruitcake mixture
250 ml (1 cup) seedless raisins
125 ml (½ cup) light brown sugar
125 ml (½ cup) white sugar
5 ml (1 tsp) bicarbonate of soda
125 g butter, roughly cubed
250 ml (1 cup) water
2 XL free-range eggs
5 ml (1 tsp) vanilla essence
15 ml (1 Tbsp) dark rum
30 ml (2 Tbsp) brandy
500 ml (2 cups) cake flour
10 ml (2 tsp) baking powder
a pinch of salt
2 ml (½ tsp) each ground cinnamon,
mixed spice and freshly
grated nutmeg
50 g glacé cherries, chopped
50 g walnuts, coarsely chopped
15 ml (1 Tbsp) finely chopped
preserved ginger

Bring the cake mixture, raisins, both sugars, bicarb, butter and water to the boil in a large, deep saucepan – it *must* be deep as the bicarb froths up. Stir and reduce the heat to low, then half-cover and simmer for 15 minutes. Cool *completely*. Whisk together the eggs, vanilla, rum and brandy. Add to the fruit mixture (in a large mixing bowl), then sift in the flour, baking powder, salt and spices. Mix well, then add the cherries, walnuts and ginger. Turn this thick, sticky mixture into a 21 x 6 cm cake tin, base and sides lined with baking paper. Smooth the top and arrange halved cherries on top, if using. Bake at 160 ℃ for 1 hour 10 minutes; test with a skewer in the centre of the cake – it should come out clean. Cool in the tin before turning out. Store airtight for a day or two before enjoying.

Chocolate-Orange Layer Cake

A large, dark cake. The ingredients are basic and it's easy to make, so it's a useful recipe and the flavour is super.

90 ml (6 Tbsp) cocoa powder
5 ml (1 tsp) instant coffee granules
250 ml (1 cup) boiling water
10 ml (2 tsp) finely grated orange rind*
4 XL free-range eggs, separated
375 ml (1½ cups) castor sugar
5 ml (1 tsp) vanilla essence
125 ml (½ cup) oil
500 ml (2 cups) cake flour
15 ml (1 Tbsp) baking powder
a pinch of salt

ICING

Vanilla butter icing, using 750 ml
(3 cups) icing sugar, sifted;
30 ml (2 Tbsp) cocoa powder;
60 ml (4 Tbsp) softened butter;
5 ml (1 tsp) instant coffee granules
dissolved in 30 ml (2 Tbsp) cold water;
5 ml (1 tsp) vanilla essence; a little
milk to moisten. Whisk everything
together until smooth.

Mix the cocoa, coffee, water and orange rind, then leave to cool. Whisk the egg yolks with the castor sugar and vanilla until the sugar has dissolved and the mixture resembles creamy butter. Add the cocoa mixture and oil, and whisk until combined. Sift in the flour, baking powder and salt, and whisk briefly, just until smooth. Fold in the stiffly whisked egg whites, using a metal spoon, then pour into 2 x 20 cm round cake tins, first brushed with oil, then base and sides lined with baking paper, and bake on the middle shelf of the oven at 180 C for about 25 minutes – do the skewer test. Leave to stand for a few minutes before inverting onto a rack. Remove the baking paper and cool, then ice and decorate with chocolate scrolls.

* When using orange rind to flavour cakes, biscuits or desserts, use firm but ripe oranges and a very fine grater – the result will be almost a pulp, and just a little will provide plenty of flavour. It is a good idea to wash the oranges in hot water first, because of the waxy coating.

Coffee & Spice Layer Cake

Despite the popular invasion of croissants and preserves, baguettes, goat's cheese and blueberry muffins with mascarpone, there's still a place, now and then, for one of those imposing iced layer cakes that used to be seen on every tea table some time in the past. Here's a reminder.

30 ml (2 Tbsp) instant coffee granules

250 ml (1 cup) hot water

125 ml (½ cup) oil

4 XL free-range eggs, beaten

5 ml (1 tsp) vanilla essence

500 ml (2 cups) cake flour

15 ml (1 Tbsp) baking powder

2 ml (½ tsp) ground mixed spice

5 ml (1 tsp) ground cinnamon

30 ml (2 Tbsp) cornflour

275 ml (1 cup plus 5 tsp) castor sugar

a pinch of salt

4 XL free-range egg whites, beaten until stiff

COFFEE BUTTER ICING

To sandwich the layers and cover the top thickly, you'll need to mix together 90 g soft butter; 750 ml (3 cups) sifted icing sugar; 5 ml (1 tsp) instant coffee granules dissolved in 15 ml (1 Tbsp) water; 2 ml (½ tsp) vanilla essence and about 15 ml (1 Tbsp) milk to moisten. Pecan nuts are optional, but they look very good on a coffee cake.

Dissolve the coffee granules in the hot water, then allow to cool down completely. Add the oil, beaten eggs and vanilla and whisk to combine. Sift the flour, baking powder, spices, cornflour, castor sugar and salt into a large mixing bowl, add the coffee mixture, and whisk quickly just until smoothly combined – do not overbeat. Using a metal spoon, fold in the egg whites in two batches. (Whisk these right at the start, and then you won't have to wash the beaters.) Turn into 2 x 20 cm round cake tins, first brushed with oil, then base and sides lined with baking paper, and bake on the middle shelf of the oven at 180 C for 30 minutes. Leave to stand for a few minutes before turning onto a rack to cool, and remove the baking paper.

Fruit & Wholewheat Buttermilk Ring Cake

This is a large, moist cake with the satisfying goodness of a sweet something made with a generous ratio of unrefined grain. Apple, nuts, carrot and honey add to the wholefood image.

250 ml (1 cup) cake flour
7 ml (1½ tsp) baking powder
7 ml (1½ tsp) bicarbonate of soda
10 ml (2 tsp) ground mixed spice
a pinch of salt
125 g soft butter*
200 ml (⅘ cup) light brown sugar
3 XL free-range eggs
375 ml (1½ cups) wholewheat flour
250 ml (1 cup) fruitcake mix OR seedless raisins
50 g walnuts, chopped
1 large, sweet apple, peeled and coarsely grated
2 medium carrots, coarsely grated
250 ml (1 cup) buttermilk
60 ml (¼ cup) oil
30 ml (2 Tbsp) runny honey
5 ml (1 tsp) vanilla essence

Sift the cake flour with the baking powder, bicarb, spice and salt. Cream the butter and sugar well. Beat in the eggs, one at a time, adding 5 ml (1 tsp) of the flour mixture with each egg. Mix the wholewheat flour, fruit mix or raisins, nuts, apple and carrot into the remaining cake flour mixture. Whisk together the buttermilk, oil and honey. Fold the flour mixture into the creamed mixture alternately with the buttermilk mixture, beginning and ending with the flour. Add the vanilla, then turn into a baking paper-lined 22 x 7 cm ring tin, spreading evenly. Place the tin on a baking tray – this is important as a ring tin usually has a removeable base and soft, oily batters such as this one will leak and drip onto the floor of the oven. Bake on the middle shelf of the oven at 180 C for 50 minutes – test with a skewer. The cake should be richly browned but will not rise to great heights due to the heaviness of the ingredients. Leave to stand for 10 minutes before turning out onto a rack to cool. The cake is moist enough to eat plain, in fat slabs, but if you wish to ice it, the best would be the icing traditionally used for carrot cakes.

* To soften butter for creaming, warm the mixing bowl with hot water, discard the water, add the cubed butter and leave for a few minutes before using.

Nutty Fruitcake Muffins

Dark and nobbly, sweet and spicy muffins. No need to butter these, they are moist enough to enjoy just as they are.

250 ml (1 cup) fruitcake mix
60 ml (4 Tbsp) butter
250 ml (1 cup) boiling water
375 ml (1½ cups) cake flour*
5 ml (1 tsp) baking powder
5 ml (1 tsp) bicarbonate of soda
a pinch of salt
7 ml (1½ tsp) ground cinnamon
2 ml (½ tsp) freshly grated nutmeg
125 ml (½ cup) wholewheat flour
125 ml (½ cup) light brown sugar
30 g walnuts, chopped
5 ml (1 tsp) vanilla essence

Place fruit mix and butter in a bowl, pour boiling water over, stir to melt the butter and leave to cool for about 15 minutes. Sift the flour, baking powder, bicarb, salt and spices, mix in the wholewheat flour, sugar and walnuts, then pour the fruit mixture into a well in the centre of the dry ingredients. Add the vanilla and mix very quickly to a lumpy batter – mix only until no trace of flour remains – then spoon into large, lightly oiled muffin cups (not paper cups), filling each to the three-quarter level. Bake on the middle shelf of the oven at 180 C for 20 minutes until brown and firm – test with a skewer to check whether they are cooked through. Leave to stand a few minutes before removing to a rack to cool. **Makes 9 large muffins.**

* White bread flour can replace cake flour and, for a more wholesome muffin, 250 ml (1 cup) wholewheat and 250 ml (1 cup) cake or white bread flour may be used instead of the above ratios.

Brown Buttermilk Muffins

... with raisins and spice and a touch of orange, all of which combine to make these a great choice to serve at a brunch, with butter and lime marmalade.

250 ml (1 cup) cake flour
a large pinch of salt
5 ml (1 tsp) bicarbonate of soda
2 ml (½ tsp) mixed ground spice
60 ml (4 Tbsp) light brown sugar
250 ml (1 cup) wholewheat flour
200 ml (⅘ cup) seedless raisins
1 XL free-range egg
60 ml (¼ cup) oil
60 ml (¼ cup) runny honey or golden syrup
250 ml (1 cup) buttermilk
5 ml (1 tsp) very finely grated orange rind

Sift together the flour, salt, bicarb and spice. Mix in the sugar, wholewheat flour and raisins. Whisk together the egg, oil, honey or syrup, buttermilk and orange rind and add this mixture to the dry ingredients; mix quickly to a lumpy batter. Spoon into large, lightly oiled muffin cups (not paper cups), filling them to the three-quarter level, and bake on the middle shelf of the oven at 180 C for 25 minutes – do the skewer test and, if done, leave to stand for a few minutes before removing to a rack to cool. **Makes 10 fat muffins.**

Rosemary-Buttermilk Scones

Plump, savoury scones topped with melted cheese – these are quite delicious served freshly baked with mid-morning coffee, with brunch, or with soup. Switch on the oven, snip the herbs, and then they're made in less time than they take to bake.

500 ml (2 cups) self-raising flour*
1 ml (¼ tsp) salt
15 ml (1 Tbsp) castor sugar
15 ml (1 Tbsp) finely chopped fresh rosemary leaves
15 ml (1 Tbsp) snipped chives
1 XL free-range egg
60 ml (¼ cup) oil
buttermilk
milk and finely grated cheddar cheese for topping

Sift the flour, salt and castor sugar and mix in the herbs. Break the egg into a measuring jug, add the oil and enough buttermilk to reach the 200 ml (⅘ cup) mark – about 125 ml (½ cup) buttermilk should just do it. Whisk these together, then add to the dry ingredients. Using a fork, mix quickly until the dough holds together, then use your hands to form into a ball. Pat out, 2 cm thick, on a lightly floured board and use a 5 cm scone cutter to cut into rounds – don't twist when cutting. Place, almost touching, on a baking tray lined with baking paper, brush the tops lightly with milk and sprinkle with cheese. Bake at 220 °C just above the centre of the oven for about 14 minutes until the scones have ballooned beautifully, are golden in colour and the cheese has melted. **Makes 10.**

* For a more wholesome scone, substitute bran-rich self-raising flour in any ratio preferred, remembering that the bran will require slightly more liquid.

Glazed Lemon Loaf

Not everyone likes iced cakes and not everyone likes fruitcakes and that's when this moist,
light and lemony loaf provides the perfect alternative.

125 g soft butter

200 ml (⅘ cup) castor sugar

10 ml (2 tsp) very finely grated
lemon rind

500 ml (2 cups) white bread flour

10 ml (2 tsp) baking powder

a pinch of salt

50 g mixed citrus peel, finely chopped

2 XL free-range eggs

250 ml (1 cup) milk

5 ml (1 tsp) vanilla essence

GLAZE

45 ml (3 Tbsp) castor sugar

90 ml (6 Tbsp) fresh lemon juice

Cream the butter, castor sugar and lemon rind until light. Sift the flour, baking powder and salt, then mix in the citrus peel. Add the eggs to the creamed butter mixture, one at a time, adding a teaspoon of the flour mixture with each egg, then add the remaining flour mixture alternately with the milk. Finally add the vanilla, give a quick whisk to even out the soft batter and turn into an oiled 19 x 8 x 7 cm loaf tin, base and sides lined with baking paper. Smooth the top to level evenly and bake at 180 C for about 50 minutes – test with a wooden skewer. Just before the end of the baking time, make the glaze by mixing the castor sugar and lemon juice in a small saucepan, stir over low heat to dissolve the sugar and then boil rapidly over high heat for a minute or two until syrupy. Remove the baked loaf from the oven but leave it in the tin. Prick the top, all over, with a thin skewer, and slowly drizzle the lemon syrup over. Leave the loaf in the tin until cold – the syrup will gradually be absorbed, and then it will be easy to turn out. Remove the baking paper. Because this loaf is so moist, it will grow mouldy if kept and should therefore be finished up within a day or two, which should not be a problem. **Makes 1 medium loaf.**

Brown Double-Ginger Loaf

If you love ginger, this is for you: it's not gingerbread as such, but a large, perfumed loaf which is delicious served sliced with soft goat's cheese (like cylinders of chevin) or cream cheese, and a preserve such as kumquat or grapefruit on the side. An unusual treat at a brunch, or tea.

125 g soft butter

200 ml (⅘ cup) castor sugar

1 XL free-range egg, lightly beaten

1 knob fresh root ginger, peeled and coarsely grated (about 15 ml (1 Tbsp))

45 ml (3 Tbsp) runny honey

45 ml (3 Tbsp) golden syrup

250 ml (1 cup) cake flour

375 ml (1½ cups) brown bread flour*

15 ml (1 Tbsp) ground ginger

5 ml (1 tsp) bicarbonate of soda

2 ml (½ tsp) baking powder

2 ml (½ tsp) ground mixed spice

200 ml (⅘ cup) milk

5 ml (1 tsp) vanilla essence

Using an electric whisk, cream the butter and castor sugar until light and fluffy. Whisk in the egg, then mix in the grated ginger, honey and syrup. Beat until thick and creamy. Sift the flours, ginger, bicarb, baking powder and mixed spice, returning the bran left in the sieve. Whisk this into the creamed mixture alternately with the milk, beginning and ending with the flour mixture, and mix to a fairly stiff batter. Finally add the vanilla. Turn into a 26 x 9 x 7 cm loaf tin, oiled and then lined, base and sides, with baking paper. (Oiling the tin first allows the paper to adhere.) Bake at 160 °C for 1¼ hours until caramel brown, risen and firm – test with a skewer. Leave to stand for a few minutes before turning out onto a rack, remove baking paper, and cool. **Makes 1 large loaf.**

* If preferred, use half cake flour and half brown flour – brown flour adds an extra fillip of fibre, but it does make a slightly heavier and less moist loaf.

Fruit & Carrot Loaf

A sweet, dense brown loaf. Serve sliced and buttered.

125 g fruitcake mixture

300 ml (1⅕ cups) water

250 ml (1 cup) light brown sugar

250 ml (1 cup) coarsely grated carrots, firmly packed for measuring

30 ml (2 Tbsp) butter

5 ml (1 tsp) ground mixed spice

250 ml (1 cup) cake flour

5 ml (1 tsp) bicarbonate of soda

5 ml (1 tsp) baking powder

a pinch of salt

250 ml (1 cup) wholewheat flour

60–75 ml (4–5 Tbsp) chopped walnuts (optional)

2 ml (½ tsp) vanilla essence

Place the fruitcake mixture, water, sugar, carrots, butter and spice in a large, deep saucepan, bring to the boil, then cover and simmer over low heat for 15 minutes. Cool completely before continuing with the recipe. Sift the cake flour, bicarb, baking powder and salt and stir into the cooled mixture in a large mixing bowl. Mix in the wholewheat flour, nuts (if using), and vanilla. Turn into a 20 x 9 x 7 cm loaf tin, first oiled and then lined, base and sides, with baking paper. Level the top and bake at 160 C for 1 hour. Test with a skewer and, if done, leave to stand for a few minutes before inverting onto a rack. Remove paper, and cool. **Makes 1 medium loaf.**

Stirred Wholewheat & Yoghurt Bread

This wholesome bread, which was once so popular, seems to be somewhat neglected now in favour of crusty, savoury Italian breads – understandable, but a pity. However, here it is again as a reminder – easy as pie, and full of good things. Despite the raisins and nuts, it's great for sandwiches as it slices thinly without crumbling – and it also makes a lovely lunch, with avo and cottage cheese and greens. The quantity of bicarb might seem very small, but it *is* enough for the bread to rise, and using this minimum amount avoids that overtly bicarb flavour that often surfaces in breads made with this ingredient as a raising agent.

250 ml (1 cup) white bread flour
7 ml (1½ tsp) salt
5 ml (1 tsp) bicarbonate of soda
750 ml (3 cups) wholewheat flour
60 ml (4 Tbsp) wheatgerm
90 ml (6 Tbsp) seedless raisins
30 g pecan nuts, chopped (optional)
500 ml (2 cups) stirred Bulgarian yoghurt (not thick, spooning yoghurt)
15 ml (1 Tbsp) oil
30 ml (2 Tbsp) runny honey
water
sesame and poppy seeds for topping

Sift the white bread flour with the salt and bicarb. Mix in the wholewheat flour, wheatgerm, raisins and nuts, if using. Whisk together the yoghurt, oil and honey, stir into the flour mixture, then add just enough water to make a sticky but *not* sloppy dough – rinse out the yoghurt carton with 100 ml (⅖ cup) water and use as much of this as necessary – you might need it all. Stir hard until thoroughly combined, then turn into a well-oiled and baking paper-lined 26 x 9 x 7 cm loaf tin, patting in evenly. Lightly press the seeds into the top and, to prevent uneven rising, make a slight depression down the centre (it will, nevertheless, hump in the oven, but it will settle down later). Bake at 180 °C for 60–70 minutes, then leave to stand for 5 minutes before loosening the sides and turning out onto a rack to cool. **Makes 1 fairly large loaf.**

Quick-Mix Herbed Buttermilk Bread

This is a jumbo loaf, humped and crusty and plump with flavour. Easy to make, as everything is simply stirred together – no rising time required – and it's super with soup or at a braai.

1 x 500 g packet self-raising flour
250 ml (1 cup) wholewheat or brown bread flour
7 ml (1½ tsp) salt
5 ml (1 tsp) sugar
10 ml (2 tsp) dried mixed herbs
3 cloves garlic, crushed
125 ml (½ cup) chopped parsley
4–6 spring onions, chopped
500 ml (2 cups) buttermilk
1 XL free-range egg
150–180 ml (⅗–¾ cup) water
grated pecorino cheese for topping

Mix all the ingredients, except the buttermilk, egg, water and pecorino. Whisk the buttermilk with the egg, add to the dry ingredients and stir to mix, then rinse the empty buttermilk carton with the water and add *just* enough to make a thick, sticky batter. The mixture needs some hard beating with a wooden spoon in order to combine, as it is heavy and dense – but it should not be sloppy, so do not add more water than is absolutely necessary. Turn into a 26 x 9 x 7 cm loaf tin, first oiled and then lined, base and sides, with baking paper. Use a dampened spatula to pat in evenly and sprinkle with pecorino, pressing it in lightly. Bake at 180 C for 1 hour – it should have risen quite dramatically and be golden brown in colour. Insert a skewer into the centre to see if the loaf is done. Leave to stand for a few minutes, turn out, remove the baking paper and return to the oven for about 5 minutes to crisp the sides, then cool on a rack. **Makes 1 very large loaf.**

Best Wholesome Bread

The recipe for yoghurt bread (page 203) is quicker to make, but this one is so economical and nutritious, you can't afford *not* to make it – the effort is minimal and the reward is great. The following quantities make a jumbo loaf which, once tried, could easily become a daily habit.

1 x 10 g packet instant dry yeast
750 ml (3 cups) wholewheat flour
500 ml (2 cups) brown bread flour
7 ml (1½ tsp) sea salt
125 ml (½ cup) sunflower seeds
45 ml (3 Tbsp) runny honey
30 ml (2 Tbsp) oil
about 600 ml (2⅖ cups) water*

* The temperature of the water is really important – warmer than luke, but not *hot* hot – a mix of boiling water and cold tap water is a rough guide.

Mix all the ingredients, except the water, in a large bowl, then mix in 250 ml (1 cup) of the water. When combined, slowly add another 250 ml (1 cup). After that, add only as much as is necessary to make a moist, springy batter – it should not be sloppy, but should have the consistency of a fruitcake batter. Turn into an oiled and lined 26 x 9 x 7 cm loaf tin. Line the base and sides with baking paper as this makes it so much easier to turn out, and level the batter with the back of a damp wooden spoon, pressing it into the tin quite firmly. Leave in a warm place until the batter reaches the top of the tin, then bake at 200 C for 30 minutes, then at 180 C for 20 minutes. Leave to stand for a few minutes before inverting onto a rack, remove the baking paper and cool, OR return to the switched-off oven for about 10 minutes to crisp the sides.

• Options: Sprinkle the top of the loaf with extra sunflower seeds (and/or sesame, or poppy seeds) before setting to rise. Add a handful of seedless raisins to the dry mixture.
• For a denser loaf, use all wholewheat flour – in this case a little more water will be necessary. Using part wholewheat and part brown flour as specified makes a larger, less heavy loaf.

Glossary

ag oh; used to express exasperation

amasi thick, soured milk

bayete Zulu royal greeting

beskuit rusks

blerrie bloody (slang)

boeretroost literally 'Afrikaner comfort'; ground coffee in a linen bag suspended in boiling water

disselbooms shafts of ox wagons to which the oxen are yoked

Dopper member of the *Gereformeerde Kerk in Suid-Afrika*, distinguishable by the short jackets worn instead of the traditional frock coat

droogtewindjie cool, drought wind

eina! exclamation of pain; ouch!

fie exclamation of distaste or mock dismay

indunas headmen or councillors apppointed by a chief

ja yes

ja-nee literally yes-no; that's a fact

katel a lightweight, portable bed; also called a trek bed

knobkieries wooden war club with a round knob at the end

koppie small hill

liefie term of affection, Afrikaans for 'lovey'

linnekas linen cupboard

Nagmaal Holy Communion, traditionally celebrated quarterly in the Dutch Reformed Church

Ons Huisie literally 'Our House'

oupa grandfather

riem a strip of softened hide used instead of rope

riempie a narrow strip of softened hide used for thonging seats and the backs of chairs

siestog an expression of sympathy or pity

sjoe! phew!

skof a stage or leg of a journey

tant aunt

velskoene literally 'hide shoes'; hand-made shoes of untanned hide

verdomde damned, accursed

vetkoek a deep-fried cake, similar to a doughnut

voorkamer the front room of a house

voorlopers usually young coloured boys, who lead a span of oxen

Index